LOCKED UP
for Eating Too Much

"Here is a work that describes searing pain, sheer hard work, and astonishing redemption. Debbie Danowski looks back from the vantage point of thirteen years of abstinence and relearns the lessons of hitting bottom. *Locked Up for Eating Too Much* belongs on the bookshelf of anyone who wants to understand the miracle of recovery."

> —Jeffrey Cain, Ph.D., Assistant Professor
> of English, Sacred Heart University

"It is rare to read something so personal and yet public. This book will touch those who read it and will result in recovery for many."

> —Genevieve Hendrix, Ph.D.

"Dr. Danowski's painfully honest story provides new insight into a problem that many people would like to deny exists. This book will make any reader stop and think about the role of food in our culture."

> —D. M. Rosner, author

"Dr. Danowski's diary is sensitive, compelling, and hopeful. Her determination is inspirational; her success is phenomenal."

> —Christopher O'Hearn, President of
> Mission College, Santa Clara, California

"This book is touching and honest. A real eye-opener for anyone affected by addiction."

> —Mark A. Egmon, President of the Association of
> Commercial Producers, Midwest Region

LOCKED UP
for Eating Too Much

◆ ►

The Diary of a Food Addict in Rehab

Debbie Danowski, Ph.D.

HAZELDEN®

Hazelden
Center City, Minnesota 55012-0176

1-800-328-0094
1-651-213-4590 (Fax)
www.hazelden.org

Library of Congress Cataloging-in-Publication Data

Danowski, Debbie, 1965–
   Locked up for eating too much : the diary of a food addict in
   rehab / Debbie Danowski.
     p. cm.
   ISBN 1-56838-793-8 (softcover)
   1. Danowski, Debbie, 1965—Diaries. 2. Compulsive eaters—
United States—Diaries. 3. Compulsive eating—Treatment—
Popular works. I. Title.

   RC552.C65 D357 2002
   616.85'26—dc21

                                    2002068635

06 05 04 03 02   6 5 4 3 2 1

Cover design by Theresa Gedig
Interior design by Ann Sudmeier
Typesetting by Stanton Publication Services, Inc.

Editor's note

All the stories in this book are based on actual experiences. In some
cases, names and details have been changed to protect the privacy
of the people involved.

   Alcoholics Anonymous is a program of recovery from alcoholism *only*—use of the Twelve Steps and other AA material in connection with programs and activities which are patterned after AA, but
which address other problems, does not imply otherwise.

   The name of the support group referred to in this book has
been withheld to protect the spirit of it.

This book is dedicated to my husband, Fred,
for giving me the courage to relive this experience.

Acknowledgments

This book would not be possible without the support and love of my family, friends, and colleagues. While it is impossible to name everyone who has contributed to this endeavor, I will attempt to acknowledge a few: my husband, Fred; my parents, Ann and Andy; my sister and brother-in-law, Karen and Danny; my niece, Melissa; my brother and sister-in-law, Mike and Denise; my husband's parents, Fred and Marie; my extended family; my friends Bev Robillard, Dawn Rosner, Mark Egmon, Jennie Hendrix, Rich Mayo, and Chris O'Hearn. I couldn't ask for more supportive and loving people to share my life with. I am grateful for each and every one of them.

God has blessed me with a wonderfully supportive working environment at Sacred Heart University, and every day I feel grateful for those people who accept me and support my efforts. I was reminded of just how much my recovery program is ingrained in not only my personal life but my professional life as well when Sacred Heart's president, Anthony J. Cernera, asked me at a recent university function if I had the food I needed. Support such as this is present at every level of the university and though I will try to identify those who have helped me, I know that it would be impossible to name everyone: Beverly Boehmke, Dr. Jeff Cain, Dr. Bunny Calabrese, Dr. Ralph Corrigan, Dr. David Curtis, Dr. Angela DiPace, Carol Esposito, Dr. Sally Michlin, Dr. Judy Miller, Teri Natale, Jocelyn Novella, Dr. Jackie Rinaldi, Dr. Roberta Staples, Dr. Sylvia Watts, and Dr. Sandy Young. Professionally, I would also like to thank Robert Galucci and his staff at the Monroe Public Library for the support they have given me.

Equally as wonderful is the support I receive from everyone at Hazelden. As a publishing company devoted to recovery and other mental health issues, Hazelden operates under the same principles that it teaches. Again, I will attempt to name a few individuals, but there are many more: Corrine Casanova, whose initial belief in me and my work marked the beginning of my writing career; Bette Nowacki, whose skillful editing made a decent manuscript into an even better one; John Ferdinand; Jody K.; MK Everts; Cathy Broberg, whose copyediting made my words come alive; Theresa Gedig for an eye-catching cover design; and Rachelle Kuehl for all of her hard work and dedication in organizing the book's production.

Additionally, the life I have today would not be possible without those people who continually support me in my recovery. Though I may never learn many of their last names, I could not have survived the past twelve years without them. Heartfelt thanks goes to Elaine, Roger, Vicki, Kim, Alex, and everyone else who regularly supports me. And, though I dare not risk naming those people who shared the summer of 1989 with me, they know who they are and exactly how important their love and support were to me even when I didn't think I needed it.

And finally, there are no words to express my gratitude to God for the life and work He has given me.

Prologue

The following pages describe my experience at a food-addiction treatment center during the summer of 1989. While there are many aspects of this true story that I am not proud of, they are the realities of my life and have contributed to making me the person I am today—a person I am proud to be. It is important to remember that the events recounted here are based on my experiences and viewpoints and aren't presented as facts. Walking into the treatment center, I was deep into my addiction and drugged up on sugar and flour. My state of mind made it impossible for me to see things objectively or even realistically. Because of this, some of the names and details about the people who shared my experiences have been changed to protect their privacy.

An experience such as this is deeply personal and to invite others to read about it is quite unnerving. Contained within these pages are the deepest, most private memories of my life. When I first recorded these thoughts, I never dreamed of sharing them with the world; even now I hesitate to do so. Yet one of the lessons I learned during the summer of 1989 is that recovery of any kind depends on other people honestly sharing their feelings without concern for the consequences. I will always be grateful to those who shared so honestly with me. I hope that in some small way my story will help someone else find recovery. Judge me as you will, but remember that many of the decisions and experiences described here took place while I suffered greatly from the effects of a devastating addiction. Though this is a fact, it is not an excuse. Today, I take full responsibility for my actions and with God's help will deal with the consequences of revealing my private thoughts and experiences.

◆ Day 1 ◆

July 3, 1989

Listening to the roar of the jet engine, I wondered what I was doing here. Why had it come to this? I turned toward the small window, searching desperately for Mark and Wendy. As if trying to find ants on a sidewalk, I studied the large windows by the gate area I had just walked through. All I could see were blobs outlined in the windows. Maybe if I just tried harder I could figure out which two were my friends. I knew they were still there. They had promised. I knew from the sympathy that had filled their eyes as I said good-bye that they wouldn't leave during this awful time. We had all come so far together. I couldn't imagine facing this without them.

A small jolt and the plane began to taxi down the runway. I could feel my heart pounding as I turned toward the windows one last time. I held my breath and closed my eyes the second I knew that I wouldn't get one last look at the friends who had helped me get here.

Biting the inside of my cheek to stop myself from crying, I loosened my grip on the seat belt now that the plane had taken off. I still wouldn't let go. The "fasten

3

seat belt" sign was still on and I couldn't risk letting the flight attendant find out that my seat belt didn't fit around me. Just a few more inches, six at the most, and it would have clicked into place. Why didn't they make these things bigger? All of my life, I had been forced to fit into a world too small for me.

I wiped one lone tear that had fallen on my cheek. What was I getting myself into? What were they going to do to me? Why me? Why couldn't I have been naturally thin like my sister? I tried not to think about this, yet I couldn't stop. My life had always been a nightmare.

By now, I should be used to the sadness that surrounded me. For all of my twenty-two years, I had been fat, really fat. The chubbiness of my childhood had quickly turned into rolls of fat hanging from every part of my body. I had sneaked into my grandmother's room to weigh myself when I was home from college last weekend—328 pounds. I really didn't think I had a problem. My counselor had said I did but I didn't believe her. I just needed to get motivated and everything would be okay.

It's true that I was miserable, but that had nothing to do with my weight. It was Tim's fault, and before him, John was to blame. Why couldn't they have loved me? If I had a problem, that was my real problem: I needed a boyfriend. What better motivation to lose weight?

From the first minute I had seen Tim outside of Mark's apartment during the second week of the fall semester at Syracuse University, I had known that he was the one who could motivate me to lose weight. With his quick smile and sparkling brown eyes, he was like no other man I had ever met. Tall, thin, and with dark, short hair, he fit the image I had of my ideal man. I had fallen in love with him almost instantly. He was so different from my first love, John. John had been rough and dangerous with a wild excitement to him, while Tim was clean-cut and open, with real goals.

Whenever Tim talked about earning his master's in business administration so that he could rule the world, my heart skipped a beat as I pictured myself by his side. I knew that if he truly did rule the world, no one would ever be able to tease me again. Of course none of that would happen now unless I could lose the weight I needed to make Tim love me. I shook my head to avoid thinking about the unpleasantness that would later follow. A loud tone alerted me that it was no longer necessary to wear my seat belt.

Whew! I sighed with relief as my fingers let go of the seat-belt latch. Since the plane was nearly empty, I had an extra seat. Quickly, I raised the seat arm that had been digging into my thigh and pushed it back between the two seats.

Within a matter of minutes, the flight attendant presented me with a breakfast tray consisting of soggy French toast, a microscopic amount of imitation maple syrup, an orange juice, and something that resembled a sausage. I didn't care what it looked like. I swallowed a large forkful of the French toast. I didn't taste anything but the sweetness of the syrup on the spongy bread. I knew that I shouldn't eat this, especially considering where I was going but what choice did I have? If I didn't eat now, who knew when I'd get something else? Taking another bite, I realized that the toast wasn't so bad after all, especially when followed by the juicy sausage.

I sure hoped that they had food at least this good where I was going. If they did, it would be okay. Food— the tastes, the smells, the chewing, the excitement of it— always made everything better. Eating was the only time life made sense. It was simple. Food tasted good so I ate it. I didn't know why I had to go somewhere like this to understand anything else.

Looking down, I surprised myself. My meal was already gone. I wanted another, but I didn't dare request more. I wanted to fool the flight attendant into believing that I was on a diet.

Studying the small houses below, I wondered about the lives of the people inside. Were they as unlucky in love as I was, or did they have nice families with children? Did they all have someone to love them, or were they alone and miserable like me?

I was glad there wasn't anyone in my row to see the tears that rolled down my cheeks. How was I ever going to get through the next six weeks? Six weeks! My God! What did they plan to do during all that time? I tried not to think about it. Instead, I concentrated on the vacation to Disney World that my sister and I had planned to take after I was done with the program. The trip would help me handle whatever they threw my way. With its magical atmosphere, Disney World could solve any problem.

Six weeks sure was a long time, though. I had never been away from home for that long. Almost every weekend I drove the five hours from school to home. I loved being back in the safety of my room with all of the food my parents made for me while I was home. Usually, I went back to school with a week's worth of food, the kind only my mother could make.

My eyelids began to feel heavy as the stress of the morning caught up with me. My flight had left at 7:35 A.M. and I wasn't used to getting up that early. Usually, I tried to sleep long into the morning, often scheduling my classes in the early afternoon or evening. I preferred to stay up late. But I wasn't that bad. I was always up by noon. My eyes closed as I felt myself drifting off to sleep. Whatever they would do in that place, I could handle it. I sighed. I had made it this far. That had to mean something.

The captain's announcement about our arrival into sunny Tampa woke me. Again, I pretended to fasten my seat belt. I smiled at the flight attendant as she walked down the aisle checking to make sure everyone had obeyed the rule. Taking a deep breath as the plane landed, I prepared myself for whatever was to happen. I had already survived a year of graduate school in a highly competitive, intensive communications program. What could be worse?

As I walked off the plane, I wasn't sure what to do. The admissions lady on the phone had said that their driver would find me. How would he know what I looked like? I worried as I scanned the waiting area. What if he didn't show up? I didn't like traveling alone.

Within minutes, I was greeted by an attractive, blond man in his late twenties, who introduced himself as Pete, the maintenance man. He explained that the regular driver's shift didn't begin until the afternoon, so he had been asked to retrieve me. After gathering my bags, we were finally on our way to Glenbeigh Hospital, which was nearly an hour's drive from the airport.

During the ride, Pete told me about his girlfriend—too bad, he was sort of cute, in a quiet, gentle way—and his life in Tampa. Glenbeigh, he told me, was close to several tourist attractions, including Busch Gardens. Well at least I could have some fun during my stay. Pete also mentioned that there was a mall close to the hospital. That's good; I was always up for shopping.

Steering the old station wagon into a large circular driveway, Pete said, "There it is."

A long, square, brick building was surrounded by palm trees, with a pond to the right of it. As Pete pulled the car up to the front entrance, I studied the building. It looked harmless enough, even resembling a few of the buildings on my college campus.

Inside, I was greeted by an admissions counselor, who promised to be brief in her inquisition of me. I had already answered countless questions about my eating patterns before I arrived, so I imagined that there wasn't much else to cover.

Ushering me into a small, sparsely furnished office, the tall, thin, blond woman seated herself behind a desk and motioned for me to sit in the wide chair facing her. Smiling, she proceeded to verify my insurance information, then instructed me to phone my parents. She wanted me to tell them that I had arrived safely and that I would speak to them again in twenty-one days.

Twenty-one days! Surely I had heard her wrong! Even though I was living five hours away from them at school, I spoke to my parents and sister almost every night. What was wrong with this woman? Didn't she have a family?

Forcing myself to smile at her, I nodded my head. For now, I would do as she asked. Later, I would find a way around this silly rule. What option did I have if I wanted to be thin for Tim? Nothing else had ever worked. I had to give this a shot.

With shaking hands, I reached for the phone and dialed my parents' number. Since my mother was usually home, I figured she would be easiest to reach. After the fourth ring, I realized she wasn't there. The counselor instructed me to try someone else, so I dialed my father's office. His secretary answered.

"He just stepped out to get lunch downstairs. He should be back in a couple minutes," she said.

Forcing myself to remain composed, I asked her to tell my father I wouldn't be able to talk with him tonight or for the next twenty-one days. I gave her a number where my parents could check on my progress. My last phone call had been to a woman I barely knew.

Then, I was escorted to the food-addiction patient unit—FAP for short—where a chubby nurse greeted me. "Here, these are for you," she said, handing me a stack of papers. "Come on. I'll show you where your room is; then we can unpack after lunch."

We? Why would I need help unpacking? How hard would it be to put a few shirts away?

Except for a few strange rules, this place seemed like any other hospital—clean, white, and sterile. The nurses wore the traditional white uniforms, and except for slightly nicer decor and queen-size beds, the rooms were standard too. Barely giving me a second to drop my bags and look around, the nurse led me to another room, behind the nurses' desk.

"Excuse me! Excuse me! I have a new girl here. Who wants to be her buddy?" The nurse's loud voice echoed throughout the huge round room with a twelve-foot sectional sofa messily arranged in a circle.

Smiling, I glanced at the others. Out of the group of thirty or so, most were women of varying weights and ages. One girl with short, red hair caught my eye as I smiled.

"I'll be her buddy," she said, returning my smile.

Though I wasn't exactly sure what a buddy was, I was grateful someone had volunteered to be mine.

"Hi, I'm Dawn. You'll need these," the girl said, handing me a set of measuring cups, a set of measuring spoons, and a small scale.

Measuring cups? What did she expect me to do with

those? The last time I had measured anything was while baking chocolate-chip cookies. I had quadrupled the recipe to make sure I had enough. Then, sure that Tim would realize what a valuable wife I would make, I had given him a heaping plateful.

As we walked toward the nurses' desk, Dawn explained that I wasn't allowed off the unit without a buddy—the hospital's term for another patient. That meant, she said, I wasn't even allowed outside by myself. Smiling, I simply nodded as we walked down the long hallway.

I glanced at the front doors as we turned right and walked through the large double doors to the cafeteria. How free I had been only seconds ago. The cafeteria struck me as very similar to the one where I was an under-graduate. I had never even seen the one at Syracuse University. Why eat there when I could be alone in my own apartment? I hated people watching me while I ate, monitoring my every bite, calculating each calorie. Who needed that? The only difference between the two cafeterias was that this one had extremely wide chairs, some of which were filled with people equally as wide.

"You can put your cups and stuff over here," Dawn directed, pointing at a round table.

Following Dawn's lead, I carried my cups and grabbed a brown plastic tray. Heading toward what appeared to be a salad bar, I watched as she began to stuff lettuce, cucumbers, peppers, and other vegetables in the eight-ounce measuring cup.

"Whatever you can fit in your cup is yours," she said, smiling as she pushed the lettuce firmly down.

Reaching for the large tongs, I gently placed several leaves of lettuce into my cup. Then, I used the smaller tongs to add cucumbers, bean sprouts, green peppers, and carrots, and I carefully balanced two cherry tomatoes on top. I poured one ladle, equaling two tablespoons, Dawn pointed out, of watery, white dressing over the vegetables.

After placing our bowls on the table, Dawn instructed me to get in the long line near the tray stand. At the end of the line, I was positioned directly in front of a wide doorway with windows. I noticed the sun glistening over the palm trees and a lone praying mantis frolicking among wood chips. As it moved away from the building, I realized that this insect had more freedom than I did.

Approaching the server, I watched as the older man in a white hat and uniform used measuring spoons and a scale to portion out green beans, corn, and something resembling meatloaf onto each plate. After he handed me mine, I filled a tan, plastic cup with ice just as I had seen Dawn do, then grabbed a can of caffeine-free cola and a small apple.

Back at our table, Dawn directed me to measure out one cup of beans, half a cup of corn, and three ounces of meatloaf. Fumbling with my fork to lift each bean into my cup, I thought how insane these people were. Why would they remeasure everything that man had already portioned out so neatly?

"Food addicts need to weigh and measure their food because after so many years of overeating, we're not sure of normal portion sizes," Dawn said while effortlessly measuring out her meal.

We? Who did she think she was including me in her sick group? By the time I had finished remeasuring my food, everything was cold, but at least some butter would make the beans bearable. Reaching for the small packet, I carefully spread it over my vegetables.

"Oh, you're supposed to measure that," Dawn reprimanded me. "You get one teaspoon at either lunch or dinner. Don't worry about it this time."

Worry about it, hell. I planned to enjoy every buttery bite of the beans. Who cared if I got a little extra butter? Looking up, I realized that a thin, dark-haired girl sitting next to Dawn had been staring at me.

"Hi, I'm Diana. Are you a porker, puker, or pooper?" she asked, smiling at me.

"What?" I smiled back as I lifted several buttery beans into my mouth.

"If you purge your food, you're a puker. If you use laxatives, then you're a pooper, but if you just binge, you're a porker."

"I'm a porker, I guess," I said smiling. Couldn't this rude girl tell that I didn't vomit or use laxatives?

By the time I had finished my lunch, I knew more about the people at my table than I wanted to. Diana, who was from Detroit, had a long history of drug use and purging her food, while Michelle from Kentucky, who was also overweight, had arrived just last night.

Reaching for my apple, I realized how much I wanted dessert. I really craved something with chocolate. Creamy, luscious candy would really make this place and these people more bearable.

After Dawn had finished eating, she showed me where to wash my measuring tools. Then we walked back to the nurses' station, where the chubby nurse instructed me to stand against the wall as she snapped a Polaroid picture of me.

"Face to the left," she said, snapping another picture before leading me to my room. Sitting on the bed closest to the door, the nurse set a clipboard on her lap.

"Okay, you can start unpacking now. First, tell me how many pair of underwear you have," she said, positioning her pencil over the plastic clipboard.

Quickly opening my suitcase and searching, I counted

my underwear. "There's seven," I said quietly. My cheeks grew hotter with each question she asked—socks, bras, jeans, shirts, and so on.

When we had finished going through my large suitcase, the nurse motioned for me to open my smaller travel bag.

"There aren't any clothes in here," I said, looking her directly in the eyes.

"We still need to go through it. There are some things that you're not allowed to have or that need to be kept behind the nurses' desk," she explained.

Repeating the process once more, the nurse instructed me to surrender my hot rollers, curling iron, mouthwash, hairspray, razors, tweezers, hair dryer, spray deodorant, aspirin, and my over-the-counter allergy pills. With the exception of the pills, I could use everything by signing them out. The items were to be held to protect myself and other patients from harm. The pills would be returned on the day I left; it seems that even allergy pills can be an addiction for some. I would be given a physical tomorrow to determine my medical needs.

Just what kind of people were these? I watched the nurse leave with my belongings. She had left me to fill out several forms and get settled in. My buddy would come to get me around 5:30 for dinner. In the stack of papers the nurse had handed me, I found a thick, tan binder with the hospital's maroon logo on the cover. Underneath, it was written, "Take the first step to wellness." Whatever that meant, I was certainly ready to be well. Setting it on the bed, I quickly placed my pants, underwear, and socks in the few drawers across from the bed, then hung my shirts in the small closet.

As I sat on the edge of the bed, I realized how exhausted I was. What I really wanted to do was take a nap. I certainly wasn't used to getting up at 5:00 A.M. Rubbing my eyes, I decided to put on my comfortable sweatpants and old shirt, instead of my tight jeans and black cotton shirt. My skin was red from the tightness of my bra and jeans.

After closing the door, I changed clothes and lay down on the huge bed. Snuggling the pillow, I buried my face deep into it. This place, not being allowed to speak with my family, the rude people, weighing and measuring my food, counting my clothes—what had I gotten myself into? Slowly rolling over, I wiped the tears from my cheeks and closed my eyes.

I awoke a few hours later and sat straight up. Glancing at my watch, I discovered it was nearly four o'clock. I hadn't even begun filling out the papers the nurse had given me. I picked up the stack and began flipping through the binder, which was divided into five sections.

The first section included a confidentiality statement that detailed my right to privacy, which was protected by federal law and regulations. Following that, an outline of patients' legal and human rights began with, "You have the right to be treated with dignity and respect; i.e., as an individual who has personal needs, feelings, preferences, and requirements." Boring.

The next page listed a five-step patient grievance procedure. Boring. Flipping ahead to the middle of the first section, I came across a list of patient rules and regulations. One paragraph was about the dress code:

> The dress code permits the wearing of casual clothes. Shoes are to be worn at all times. Men are to wear shirts buttoned. No tank tops while in lectures, group meetings, in the Dining Room, or during scheduled activities, except recreational

activities are permitted. Women should not wear tank tops or halters. If shorts are worn they should be street clothes and not the beach variety; i.e., "short-shorts," cut-offs, or running/soccer shorts. Sweat suits and warm-up suits should be worn for recreational use only.

I set the binder down and changed back into my tight jeans and black shirt. I didn't want to break a rule, especially not this early into my stay.

Next, I began filling out the paperwork. The forms resembled exams I had taken at school—the multiple-choice kind in which the dots had to be filled in completely or the computer couldn't read the answers. Only here the questions were very personal. Had I ever thought of suicide? Yes. Did I often count things randomly? Yes. How often did I feel depressed? Often. Had I ever attempted to harm myself? No. Was there a history of alcoholism in my family? Yes.

For the next hour, I concentrated on answering the questions as honestly as I could, never stopping until I heard a knock at the door.

"It's time for dinner," Dawn smiled, as she poked her head into my room. "Don't forget your cups and scale."

I walked to the lounge and retrieved my cups, scale, and spoons from the cubbyhole I had been assigned. Then I met Dawn by the nurses' station. I noticed that her eyes were red and swollen. I asked if she was okay. Nodding her head, she held the large, metal door open to the cafeteria.

Standing in the doorway, I watched the thirty or so people weighing and measuring their food, again wondering what I had gotten myself into. I surely wasn't as bad off as the rest of these people. Sure, I was a little overweight, but nothing serious, certainly not serious enough to be locked up with these people. But, as Dawn had just told me, my options were severely limited at this point.

If I left this place AMA (against medical advice), my insurance company wouldn't pay for even one day of my stay. At more than $800 a day, I couldn't afford an hour in this place. Before I left home, my father had made it clear to me that he wouldn't pay a dime for my stay here. Having spent thousands of dollars on my dieting attempts through the years, he had finally put his foot down. Without any other source of income, I was trapped here.

Quietly, I turned and walked toward the salad bar, tightly clenching my measuring cups. If I was going to survive here, I'd have to follow the rules. I couldn't imagine what would happen if I didn't.

◆ Day 2 ◆

July 4, 1989

It is with a profound sense of irony that I celebrate Independence Day in this place. There's certainly no freedom here. From the minute I was awakened at 6:00 A.M., every hour of my day was planned. It was hard to even find time to go to the bathroom!

I was told to be in the lounge by 6:45 A.M. for "Meditation." The lounge is what they call the room behind the nurses' station. After dressing as quickly as I could, I looked over the day's schedule. After meditation, at 7:45, there was something called "Leisure Counseling," followed at 8:45 by "Gentle Eating," which lasted until 9:30.

Next on the schedule, at 9:45 A.M., was "First Step" until 11:00, when "Family Group" took place. I didn't have to worry about that one. My family was thousands of miles away. Maybe they'd give me some free time.

Almost two hours later when family group was finished, it would be lunchtime, followed by "Orientation, Education" or "Men's Body Image." Thank God, I wasn't a man. Who wanted to think about body image?

By 3:00 P.M., I was expected to be in "Recovery Group"

or "Journal," whatever they were. "Recreation" was next, followed by dinner, then at 6:45 P.M., a "Step Meeting." At 9:00 P.M., it would be time for "Metabolic Adjustment," which I had learned was a fancy name for a snack consisting of two tablespoons of oat bran and one tablespoon of wheat germ, a cup of skim milk, and an apple. I had done the same thing last night. With a little cinnamon and a package of artificial sweetener—we are allowed six a day—the cereal wasn't bad, even if it did look like birdseed.

At 10:30 P.M., all patients were expected to be in their rooms. An hour later, lights had to be out. Last night, I had gone to sleep right after "Metabolic." I certainly didn't want to be awake any longer than I had to and since I didn't have a roommate, there was no one to bother me. I was grateful for my time alone.

I had no idea how I was going to do all of the things on this schedule. I couldn't remember the last time I had been up for sixteen hours straight, never mind being this busy. A thin person with a lot of energy definitely came up with this schedule.

After reading about the day ahead of me, I felt exhausted as I headed toward the lounge. I didn't want to be here anymore. What I wanted more than anything was to go home and see Tim. I wanted things to be the way they used to be. So what if his baseball cards and computer were more important to him than I was? Maybe I could be happy being in third place. If I just tried harder, maybe he would love me. Why did I think about him so much? Shaking my head, I forced myself to think about other things. If I was going to survive here, I had to pay attention to what was going on.

Before opening the door to the lounge, I took a deep

breath. I had no idea what was going to happen in there.
I only hoped that I was strong enough to handle it. Walking in, I saw a dozen people scattered on the sofa sections.
Some were talking quietly, while others looked as if they
were sleeping.

I scanned the crowd for Dawn, but I didn't see her. I
did see Diana, the rude girl from lunch. I purposely took
a seat across the room from her. I certainly didn't want to
talk to her again. I saw an older woman with gray hair
sitting next to a man in his early forties. Other than two
slimmer girls, I seemed to be the youngest one in the
room. At least there were a lot more women than men.
I had only seen four since I got here. Next to me was a
chubby girl with long orangish-blond hair. As I sat down,
she smiled at me.

"Hi. I'm Paulette. You're new, aren't you?" she asked.
I nodded my head.

"Well, don't worry. This is one of my favorite things
here. It's not at all like family group. You don't even have
to say anything if you don't want to. Where are you
from?"

"Connecticut . . . eerrhh . . . I go to school in Syracuse,
New York, but I grew up in Connecticut and I'll go back
there after I graduate. What about you?" I returned her
smile.

"Montana."

"How long have you been here?" I asked, noticing
that her whole face seemed to shine.

"Almost two weeks, and it's really been great. I love it
here. I'm away from my husband and kids. This is my
time to work on myself. I really—"

"Okay, everyone! Let's get started!" a tall, dark-haired
woman yelled, as she locked the door.

"If you don't get here on time, they take away one day of your phone privileges after your twenty-one days," Paulette leaned over and whispered to me.

Reading from one of the books I had been given yesterday, the dark-haired woman talked about being grateful for what we have.

Grateful? At 7:00 A.M., I was sitting in a room full of strangers listening to a sermon. Breakfast was almost two hours away and my stomach was growling. The only thing I'd be grateful for was some food. My eyes began to close as she droned on.

When she was done, everyone gathered in a circle and said a prayer. Someone said, "I wish special love and energy to my family back home. I miss them and hope they are doing okay." When she finished, I nearly yelled because I already missed talking to my family so much. The worst experience of my life and I couldn't even tell them about it.

After a few more people wished "special love and energy" to people in their lives, we were released to our next scheduled activity. Paulette told me that "Leisure Counseling" meant a walk outside or aerobics.

I followed Paulette out of the meditation room. At the nurses' station, she reached for a clipboard to sign out to go outside. Then she asked one of the nurses, "Can she walk too?"

The nurse looked me up and down before asking, "Did you have your physical yet?"

"No," I held my breath after speaking.

Sighing, the nurse hesitated before saying, "Okay, but no running. Only slow walking until you see the doctor."

Smiling at Paulette, I followed her down the long hallway to the double set of glass doors. Running? Who was that woman kidding? Why would I ever want to do that?

The cool morning air felt wonderful as I took a deep breath. Following Paulette to an asphalt path around the pond, I noticed that the palm trees looked especially green.

As we walked, she talked, but I couldn't concentrate on what she was saying. All I could hear was the roar of engines from cars whizzing by on the nearby street. Did those drivers know how lucky they were to be free? Looking at all of the cars in the parking lot, I suddenly missed my own black Buick Somerset. I just wanted to get in it and drive as far away from this place as I could. I wanted to tell them what to do with their schedule and their meditation and just leave.

"I'm not sure how much longer my husband's insurance will cover my stay here. They haven't committed to the whole six weeks yet," Paulette looked at me. "I really hope they do."

Her words had snapped me back to reality. The total for my stay here was already $1,600! I didn't have that kind of money. The longer I stayed here, the bigger the lock on my cage became. The most I could hope for was that my insurance coverage would run out. I smiled at Paulette and nodded.

I thought Paulette was crazy for wanting to stay here, but she did seem nice enough. I was drawn to her gentleness. It made me miss my mother even more. My mother had always been the one I turned to whenever the teasing at school got too bad to handle. Though I never told her what had happened, it was as if she knew.

By the time 8:45 rolled around, I was more than ready to eat. I met up with Dawn, who told me not to bring my scale. I wouldn't need it for breakfast. At least that was something positive. Once inside the cafeteria, Dawn instructed me to get one cup of cereal. There were several choices but she said Sunflakes was one of the best. I decided to try that. Next, she handed me an eight-ounce container of skim milk. Yuck!

Dawn explained that on Mondays, Wednesdays, and Fridays, we could have eggs if we ordered them the night before. Since I hadn't, I could have either a half-cup of nonfat, plain yogurt or a quarter-cup of nonfat cottage cheese. They both sounded disgusting to me, but I was no fool. I chose the yogurt. A half-cup was more than a quarter-cup.

Finally, Dawn told me that I could have either one fruit—a small apple or small orange—or one cup of mixed fruit, such as melons, blueberries, or strawberries. Dawn recommended the blueberries and strawberries mixed together on top of the yogurt. Though I doubted her, I decided to take her advice for lack of a better plan. Also at her suggestion, I added one package of artificial sweetener to the cereal and another to the fruit mixture.

Just as I finished measuring everything, the lights were turned off and a small blond woman came in and directed everyone to close their eyes. Close our eyes! I was starving. For the next ten minutes she played soft music and read to us from a book. We were instructed to sit quietly and breathe deeply. With each breath I took, I smelled the sweetness of the blueberries. I couldn't wait to eat them, but I didn't dare. I had no idea what the penalty would be for acting out of order.

Finally, just as I was about to crack, the counselor told us to open our eyes and eat slowly. She said there was no talking and that we had to put our spoon down between each bite.

"Chew slowly. Be gentle with your food. Look at each other and smile. You need to learn to eat slowly. It takes twenty minutes for your body to get the message that you're full. Give yourself that time." She closed her book and left.

This was truly the most idiotic thing I had ever done. I hardly even tasted the food. I felt like a moron sitting there with my spoon down while I chewed and smiling at other people whom I didn't even know. I had never spent that much time with so many people in silence.

After I had finished as quickly as I could, Dawn directed me to wash out my measuring cups and then go into the room across from the lounge. "First Step" was next. Grabbing a chair in the back of the circle, I watched as everyone piled in and took a seat. Sitting next to the woman who had done the reading this morning was an older, dark-haired woman. Her eyes were red and her face was flushed, but she wasn't that overweight.

"Okay everyone. Let's start with the Serenity Prayer," Linda B., the counselor from this morning, said.

"God, grant me the serenity to accept the things I cannot change, the courage to change the things I can, and the wisdom to know the difference," the group recited in unison.

"Tammy?" Linda turned to the dark-haired woman.

"My name is Tammy and I'm a food addict. I feel nervous, scared, terrified, and anxious."

"Hi, Tammy," the group responded.

"I was born a food addict. Food has always been a problem in my life for as long as I can remember. I ate whatever I could without being caught. . . ."

For the next twenty minutes, Tammy talked about how food had ruined her life. She said she had always been certain that her eating had only affected her, but now she knew that was wrong.

"There were so many times when I was mean to my

children because all I wanted to do was be left alone to eat. And, my poor husband, I never wanted to be with him because I was so fat. All I cared about was eating. I even got into a car accident because I was eating while I was driving. I could have died because food was so important to me." Tammy began to cry, but despite that, she continued talking for several more minutes about how awful her life had been.

When she was done, other patients raised their hands to share their feelings about food. I couldn't believe these people were saying such things out loud. Didn't they know such thoughts were supposed to be kept to themselves? I wanted to run out of the room and go as far away as I could, but I was afraid of the punishment that would follow.

I simply sat there listening as other people told of their bad relationships with family members, their binges, and their feelings of self-hatred and disgust. What kind of people were these? Was I in danger of being hurt during one of their emotional outbursts? They seemed so emotional. They were out of control. Their lives were so messed up. I wasn't like them, so why was I here? Except for this weight thing, my life was fine, not like these people's.

Thankfully, when the session was over, I was told not to go into family group because the doctor was ready to give me a physical. I was never so happy in my life to see a doctor. I hate going to a doctor, but this was ten times better than the alternative. Who knew what they did in family group.

With a nurse standing by, the male doctor listened to my heart, examined my breasts, pushed on my stomach, and took my blood pressure. Since he didn't seem shocked by any of the readings, I figured I was in good

health. Maybe I didn't need to lose weight. I didn't seem
to have any of the physical problems these people did.
Tammy had talked about having diabetes and someone
else had mentioned heart trouble. I didn't have these
problems, so why bother going to all of this trouble?
Maybe after my physical, they would let me out early.

But I wouldn't think about that right now because it
was lunchtime. Lunch was pretty much a repeat of yesterday, except without the butter—yuck! It was after
lunch in journal group where things got worse. Going
around the circle, we each had to introduce ourselves by
saying our names, addictions, and feelings. I hated speaking in front of other people. In classes, I did whatever it
took to hide myself and remain silent. As each person
spoke, it drew nearer to my turn. I tried to listen to what
they were saying, but my heart pounded so loudly that I
thought I was going to throw up. They were only two
people away from me. What would I say?

As the girl next to me finished, I could feel everyone's
eyes look in my direction. My face reddened as I said quietly, "My name is Debbie and I'm a food addict. I feel
nervous." Just as I finished, tears fell on my cheeks and I
began to sob quietly. I tried to stop but I couldn't. I could
feel more tears fall as I swallowed hard, wiped my cheeks,
and forced myself to smile. I felt so stupid, but at least no
one left the room. I'm still not sure what I was crying
about. After that, I could barely concentrate on what the
others were saying as they read from their journals. I just
kept thinking about how embarrassed I was. I couldn't
remember ever crying before in front of anyone, never
mind a group of thirty people.

During journal group, I learned that every day I have
to answer questions in a journal, which is in the big
binder I was given my first day. Since I didn't do my

assignment yesterday, I'm already behind. I certainly
don't want to make them mad here. Who knows what
they would do? I spent the rest of the day thinking about
the questions. Luckily, there wasn't anything else that
I had to concentrate on. Unfortunately, tomorrow I will
have to attend family group. I feel nauseated by the
thought of it.

Well, either way, I had better get started. Yesterday's
entry said to read "The Doctor's Opinion" in the book *Alcoholics Anonymous,* also called the AA Big Book, changing all references to "alcohol" and "alcoholism" to "food"
and "food addiction" in my mind.

It took awhile to locate the book from the big stack
they handed me yesterday. But after I read the eight
pages, I'm supposed to answer three questions. I think
they're expecting too much, asking me to write something each day in addition to attending so many groups.

Well, I had better get started on the questions. Morning, especially 6:00 A.M., will come soon enough. Hopefully, the worst of it is over, except, of course, for family
group. I am very afraid of that and I know tomorrow the
doctor won't be there to rescue me again.

The first question asks what I related to in the reading.
The first phrase from the reading that I "relate to" is
"once having lost their self-confidence, their reliance
upon things human, their problems pile up. . . ." I know
from talking with my counselor before I came here that I
have relied on food instead of other people to deal with
my problems.

The other line that stands out to me in the reading
about people's "allergy" to alcohol (oops, I mean "food")
is ". . . their alcoholic [food-addiction] life seems the only
normal one." My life before I came here and as I was grow-

ing up seemed normal to me. Being here does not. I do not understand many things here, especially the concept of a "Higher Power."

The next question is whether my food addiction is as serious as alcoholism. After being with the people here, I'm starting to think my food addiction may be more serious than I had thought. Why else would they even have a place like this?

I do relate to the addiction aspects of the chapter. I especially understood the part about the "sense of ease and comfort which comes at once by taking a few drinks [eating]. . . ." I always feel happy when I'm eating something sweet.

The last question is about the issues I wish to work on today. I want to work on just staying here and sharing the incredible amount of fear I have about the program. It seems as if everyone here thinks the same. What if this turns out to be something like those crazy religious cults? Will I be brainwashed too?

Now that I've completed yesterday's questions, I can move on to today's assignment. I'm to reread "The Doctor's Opinion" where it discusses clearing your brain, then discuss the steps I've taken to do that so I can "set into acceptance and let go of control."

The biggest action I've taken is to remain here even though I want to leave. This morning I was allowed to walk around the pond with the others. When I was out there, I just wanted to keep on going but I didn't. I hate getting up at 6:00 A.M. and being on such a rigid schedule, but to help with this I've started talking with other people besides my "food buddy."

Also, I shared how afraid I am in journal group, where some people read their answers to these questions. If you get called on to read and you haven't done your work, you lose one day of phone privileges. That would mean twenty-two days instead of twenty-one!

Another thing I'm doing that's good, according to the rules, is that I'm doing this work in the lounge with others. I'm not staying in my room, even though I really want to. Someone told me that part of the "disease" of food addiction is to isolate yourself.

The next question is to write about the things I understand better than I did yesterday: Today when Tammy read her First Step, I could relate to a lot of what she said. She would rather have spent time alone with food than with her family or friends and that had gotten her into a car accident because she was eating and not paying attention. Last year, I got a speeding ticket because I had no idea how fast I was going while searching desperately for my roast beef sandwich. The cop had been following me for nearly a mile.

After hearing Tammy's confessions, I am more convinced that I belong here, though I still doubt it and want to go home. I'm tired of these people and their problems. Why don't they just shut up and get on with things?

The next questions ask how I feel about the actions I have had to take to stop bingeing. Why do they keep asking me that? I feel ashamed, embarrassed, and still doubtful and distrustful of the program. And I miss my family, friends, and, of course, Tim. I wonder what he's doing.

Once again, the final entry asks me to write about the issues I want to work on today. I guess I should start working on the way I concentrate on what my "friend" is doing in the outside world while I'm here. It's much easier to worry about him than it is to think about what's happening here.

From listening to another woman read her journal entry today, I learned that I'm thinking about Tim to distract myself from my feelings about being here. Maybe that's true. But who wants to feel the sheer terror of being locked up here not knowing what's going to happen next?

July 5, 1989

Today, I met with my individual counselor. Her name is Linda, but not the Linda from yesterday. Linda P., as my counselor is known, has been abstinent from sugar, flour, and caffeine for six years. She's rumored to be the toughest therapist on the FAP unit.

Well, at least I didn't get the guy counselor. It's bad enough that he heads my small family group each day. One male counselor on the entire unit and I get him for my group. It's still better than having him for my individual counselor. I couldn't imagine sharing my deepest thoughts with a man.

In the meeting with Linda, we talked a lot about how I feel about myself. It was sort of weird. I mean, what does she expect? At 328 pounds, I couldn't possibly like myself. How could she even expect that?

Now, whenever I introduce myself, which happens at each group meeting, I have to say that I'm lovable and likable. That means, in addition to saying I'm a food addict, which is required of everyone, and stating how I feel, I have an extra sentence.

My introduction is now, "My name is Debbie. I'm a food addict and I'm likable and lovable. I feel (fill in the blank)." I better practice this one. How am I supposed to remember all of this?

I have noticed, though, that my memory has already improved in the few days that I haven't eaten sugar, flour, or caffeine. They say here that food addicts are physically addicted to sugar, flour, and caffeine in the same way alcoholics are to alcohol.

I'm not sure I buy it, but I certainly do feel better. My mind seems clearer and I have a lot more energy. And, in all honesty, I don't crave food, but that's probably because I don't have much time to think about it with this hectic schedule.

It seems I'm lucky. Some people are so sick with withdrawal from sugar, flour, and caffeine that they can't get out of bed. That just proves that I'm not as bad off as most of the people here. Maybe they have an early release program I can become eligible for.

I'm trying to do everything perfectly so they will leave me alone. I certainly don't want to be called on to discuss my feelings about food. I feel great about eating it. What more is there to say?

The most terrifying thing I did today was go to family group, which they call small family group because patients break into several little groups. I was so sure that I could get out of it since my family is so far away. They explained, however, that the purpose of the group is to share our feelings with each other as we would in a family environment.

After Linda P. told me about my group assignment, she directed me to the exercise room, where my group would meet at 11:00 A.M. *sharp.* No one was allowed to leave the room during the ninety-minute session, no matter what. Even going to the bathroom was not allowed. Having heard all of this, I wanted to go even less than before, if that was possible.

At 10:55, I walked into the small room, my heart racing. Other than a wall of mirrors, an exercise bicycle, and a weight bench, the room resembled all of the others. I chose a chair across the room to make sure my back was to the mirrors and sat down.

As other patients started to walk into the room, I had the urge to run and hide. I didn't want to see these people and I didn't want to do whatever it was they did in here. Even Paulette had said she didn't like this group, and she liked this place. As I felt my heart pounding wildly, voices in my head were screaming, "Get out! Leave now!" The more people who came in the room, the louder the voices screamed.

I knew I couldn't listen to them. If I did, I would never be thin and never have a chance with Tim. Not only would I be lonely, but with the prices here I would be bankrupt as well. Forcing myself to breathe deeply, I watched as two men—one heavyset with dark hair and the other pathetically thin with a long dirty-blond beard and glasses—took seats directly across the circle from me.

Next, three women walked in. One was older with cropped gray hair. While she was slightly chubby, she didn't look too overweight. I would have killed to be her weight. The most striking thing about her was her deep blue eyes. They seemed to be constantly smiling, no matter what her facial expression.

One of the other women, who looked to be middle-aged, seemed to be exactly the opposite of the first. Though her hair was short too, it was washed-out blond.

Her face was drawn, she looked pale, and the excess weight she carried was in her hips and thighs. She looked like a giant pear.

The last woman, however, was completely different from the other two. She was a young woman with sunshine-colored straight hair that she wore in a long bob. Her face, while beautiful, was cold and hard. She was extremely overweight and she wore the usual fat clothes—polyester stretch slacks and a coordinating short-sleeved shirt. At least I had never done that. I had always made sure to wear jeans. That just proved that I wasn't as sick as she was. I could still fit into jeans, and the kind without elastic at the waist. It's true that I was in the biggest size they made—forty-eight—without having to resort to the elastic, but they still fit.

A glance at my watch told me that group would begin in exactly two minutes. The last woman to enter the room was a dark-haired girl who looked about the same age as me. She had braces on her teeth and she was thin. I wondered what she was doing here. She looked perfect. Her calves were thin and she was shapely. The only thing that looked wrong with her was her eyes. They were red and swollen. She held a hand over her face and avoided looking anyone in the eyes as she took the seat to the right of me.

Just then, I saw a tall, thin man with glasses come in. He smiled at the group before he reached for the door to close it. He had it about halfway closed when all of a sudden I saw Paulette grab the door and push her way past him.

"Sorry," she said. "I just came from meeting with Theo and we ran late."

She smiled at the counselor, then quickly took the

empty seat next to me. When she saw me, she smiled and mouthed, "Don't worry, it will be okay." That made me even more nervous. Why did she feel it necessary to reassure me?

"Okay, let's get started," the man said as he took the only empty seat. Everyone joined hands, hesitated a second, and recited, "God, grant me the serenity to accept the things I cannot change, the courage to change the things I can, and the wisdom to know the difference."

"Who wants to begin?" the man asked.

"I will," said the gray-haired woman with the sparkling eyes. "My name is Ramona and I'm a food addict. I feel happy, excited, and grateful."

"Hi, Ramona," the group responded in unison.

"Next," the counselor said.

"I'm Brian and I'm a food addict, a codependent, and I'm powerless over my anger. I feel angry and frustrated," the heavyset, dark-haired man said.

"Hi, Brian."

"My name is Ernie. I'm a food addict and addicted to exercise. I feel sad."

"Hi, Ernie."

"I'm Patti and I'm a food addict and codependent. I feel misunderstood," the fat blond-haired woman said.

"That's not a feeling," the man said. "That's a judgment. Tell us how it feels to be misunderstood."

"Bad," Patti replied.

"No. Stick to the five basics—sad, mad, glad, happy, or afraid."

"Sad."

"Okay, next," the counselor said.

"I'm Beth and I'm a food addict and a codependent. I feel sad and embarrassed."

"Hi, Beth."

"My name is Phil and I'm a food addict and codependent. I feel happy and grateful," the counselor said when it was his turn.

"Hi, Phil."

After Phil introduced himself, I realized there was only one girl before it was my turn. My heart pounded as I forced myself to listen.

"My name is Tracy and I'm a food addict, a bulimic, and a codependent. I feel sad, scared, and angry."

"Hi, Tracy."

"My name is Debbie," my voice cracked as I tried to remember everything I was supposed to say. "I'm a food addict and I'm likable and lovable. I feel good." Tears rolled down my cheeks.

"Okay, try again. *Good* is a judgment about your feelings. Remember, sad, mad, glad, happy, or afraid," Phil said gently.

"I . . ." I thought for a second as I felt my cheeks burning. "I feel afraid." Then I could control it no longer. I sobbed hysterically. As tears wet my cheeks, I covered my face quickly.

"It's okay to be afraid. When I get scared, I need to reach out to someone else," Phil said as he grabbed Tracy's hand. "It helps me to know that I'm not alone."

I nodded as he turned toward Paulette.

"My name is Paulette and I'm a food addict and a codependent. I am worthy of love. I feel anxious and grateful."

"Hi, Paulette."

"Who wants to do some work today?" Phil looked around the circle. "Tracy, do you have an assignment?"

"Yes," she said softly. "Ten reasons why I hate my disease."

"Okay, let's begin then," Phil said.

"Number one, it took away my life. Number two, I missed my prom because of it. Number three, I hate myself because of it. Number four, I don't have any friends. . . ." Tracy stopped as the tears rolled down her cheeks. She began to sob heavily. I couldn't believe that no one reached out to comfort her. These people really were cold.

"What's going on?" Phil asked. "Tell us what you're feeling."

"I feel sad, so very sad. . . ." Tracy continued to cry and her body shook.

For someone so pretty and thin, she sure seemed to have a lot of problems. She looked like one of those cheerleaders I had hated in high school, the ones who seemed to be so popular with the guys.

"Keep reading," Phil demanded.

"Number five, it made me lose my job. Number six, I lost my boyfriend because of it. Number seven, my family hates me. Number eight . . ." Tracy took a deep breath and wiped the tears away from her face. "I feel fat all of the time. Number nine, I lost so many years of my life locked up in eating-disorder hospitals. Number ten, I had to leave college because of it." Tracy began to cry even harder. A low moan escaped from her body as she bent over sobbing.

Who has some feedback for Tracy?" Phil asked.

"I do," Ramona said.

As I turned in her direction, I wiped a few tears from my cheeks. Surely this woman would know what to say to this distraught girl.

"I hear a lot of self-pity and blame."

All this woman could say to this poor girl was that she heard self-pity and blame?

"Good. Who else has some feedback for Tracy? Brian?"

"Tracy, I feel angry. I could relate to a lot of what you said and I feel mad about all of the things in my life that my disease has taken away. I almost lost my wife because of this. My career is in a shambles and I'm almost a hundred pounds overweight, all because of this fucking disease. Yet, I didn't hear any of that anger from you. I heard self-pity."

"Anyone else?" Phil asked.

"I could relate to what you said, Tracy," Beth said. "I have lost so much time to this disease. It's awful and I hate it."

Beth began to cry and tears also fell on Tracy's cheeks once again.

"There's a lot of self-pity going on here," Phil said. "In order to recover, I need to get past feeling sorry for myself. That doesn't do me any good. I have a disease, but I am not my disease and I can't blame myself for that. If I do, I remain stuck in my disease. Self-pity is one of the things that I'll eat over, so I need to be very careful about it. You need to get through this, Tracy. You need to feel the anger." Phil clenched his fist. "Doesn't it make you angry that your disease took so much of your life away from you?"

The more he talked, the more I could feel my cheeks turning red. I hated being fat. I couldn't stand the way people looked at me, but how could this thin girl know about any of that?

"Who wants to go next?" Phil asked. No one raised their hands for several seconds until Ramona finally did.

"I'll read my gratitude list," she said, smiling. "I'm grateful to be abstinent. I'm grateful for being given my life back. I'm grateful that I'm able to think clearly and remember things. I'm grateful that I can move around so much easier. I'm grateful for . . ."

She continued reading for a few more minutes about how wonderful her life was. But, if that was true, what was she doing here?

The remainder of the group session was devoted to Beth. Her assignment had been to write an anger letter to her husband. He sounded like a horrible man. She said that he always criticized her and told her how fat she was. Tim had never done that. The more she read, the redder her face turned.

Phil handed her a pillow and she knelt down on the floor. She banged the pillow against the floor as she yelled at her husband. Her nose was running and she was sweating. It looked ridiculous, but she kept on yelling, all the while beating the pillow against the ground. And when she was done, almost everyone told her what a good thing she had done.

Wonderful? She looked insane to me. Why would someone make such a spectacle of herself? These people were even weirder than I had imagined. Through it all, I simply sat there and watched even though I wanted to bolt from the room. I hated loud noises, and Beth's yelling was definitely one of the loudest I had ever heard. I wasn't going to let them beat me, though. I knew I had to sit there and that's what I did until Phil finally told us it was time to end.

Thankfully, lunch was next. Some food and a few easier groups the rest of the day helped me to partially forget how much I had hated watching Beth make such a fool out of herself. The worst part was that I had to go back there tomorrow.

Why couldn't Tim be here to take me away from all

of this? I missed him so much and I couldn't even call Mark, our mutual friend, to see what was happening in Tim's life. I wouldn't dare call Tim himself after what he had said to me. My heart ached to talk to someone I cared about. I wanted to call my parents and ask them to get me out of this crazy place. I wanted to tell them how much I missed them and that I loved them. After hearing so many horrible stories in here, I was reminded that I was one of the lucky ones. My parents had never beaten me or anything like that.

Thinking about them only made me hate this place even more. I longed for the security of my basement bedroom, where I had spent so many nights eating potato chips dunked in chocolate-chip ice cream. That was the safest place I knew. Nothing in here felt safe.

I better get to my journal questions. They want me to read "The Doctor's Opinion" again (groan) and discuss my "allergies." I guess I am "allergic" to food—sugar, flour, and caffeine.

I am definitely "allergic" to potato chips. I can never eat just one, but who can? I eat them when I feel lonely or unloved or when I want safety. I ate them when I found out that Tim didn't have romantic feelings for me. I felt sad, lonely, unloved, abandoned, and angry. I binged on a huge bag of potato chips, a half-pound of M&M's, four hot dogs, and a hamburger.

The next question says to write about self-reliance, self-confidence, and insolvable problems: When I think of self-reliance, I feel scared, pressured to perform, and very bitter. With self-confidence, it's anxious, uptight, envious, and tense. And insolvable problems make me feel stupid, powerless, scared, and angry.

Again, the last question asks about the issues I wish to work on today: I want to accept that I belong here and that I am a food addict. The group meeting today motivated me to look at this even more. Listening to these people talk about their problems with food really makes me think. I have done some of the things they talk about—hiding food, lying about what I've eaten, and isolating myself to eat.

Then, this afternoon when I was talking with another new patient, I realized that I am not alone in my confusion. She has no idea what's going on either. But I have an advantage. I've been here one more day than she has. That means I only have eighteen more days until I can call my family! I wrote them a letter yesterday, begging for cards, letters, flowers, or anything to help ease the loneliness.

I also want to accept that I am lovable and likable. I feel really stupid saying that each time I introduce myself. I'm always afraid that the other patients are going to think I'm conceited and not talk to me.

Someone—I can't even remember her name—said at the evening group meeting that pages 448 to 449 of the *Alcoholics Anonymous* book help her accept things. I'm going to try reading this each night before I go to bed:

> At last, acceptance proved to be the key to my drinking [food] problem. After I had been around A.A. for seven months, tapering off alcohol and pills, not finding the program working very well, I was finally able to say, "Okay, God. It *is* true that I—of all people, strange as it may seem, and even though I didn't give my permission—really, really am an alcoholic [food addict] of sorts. And it's all right with me. Now, what am I going to do about it?" When I stopped living in the problem and began living in the answer, the problem went away.

From that moment on, I have not had a single com-pulsion to drink [eat].

And acceptance is the answer to *all* my problems today. When I am disturbed, it is because I find some person, place, thing, or situation—some fact of my life—unacceptable to me, and I can find no serenity until I accept that person, place, thing, or situation as being exactly the way it is supposed to be at this moment. Nothing, absolutely nothing happens in God's world by mistake. Until I could accept my alcoholism [food addiction], I could not stay sober [abstinent]; unless I accept life com-pletely on life's terms, I cannot be happy. I need to concentrate not so much on what needs to be changed in the world as on what needs to be changed in me and my attitudes.

Shakespeare said, "All the world's a stage, all the men and women merely players." He forgot to mention that I was the chief critic. I was always able to see the flaw in every person, every situation. And I was always glad to point it out, because I knew you wanted perfection, just as I did. A.A. and acceptance have taught me that there is a bit of good in the worst of us and a bit of bad in the best of us; that we are all children of God and we each have a right to be here. When I complain about me or about you, I am complaining about God's handi-work. I am saying that I know better than God.

I'm not sure I get all of this passage, but I feel calm after reading it, so why not do it each night? It certainly couldn't hurt and it will probably be the easiest thing I'll do here.

◆ Day 4 ◆

July 6, 1989

At least today I was a little calmer than yesterday, as calm as I can be here. The constant state of panic that I'm in is the worst. I feel as if I'm living under a microscope. Whatever I do, wherever I am, doctors, nurses, counselors, or other patients are observing me every minute, and I'm so afraid of doing something wrong.

The punishment, or the consequence as they tell us to call it, for violating a rule is the loss of a day's phone privileges. Nothing scares me more than that. I really think I would die if that happened. I've never been out of contact with my family and friends this long. I can hardly even think about Tim without feeling horribly sad, even though he said those mean things to me. It's almost as if I'm afraid that they can read my mind here, so I'm trying not to think about him and I certainly won't talk about him. I don't intend to get that close to these people.

I heard some of the patients saying that the nurses report back to the counselors about what we do. How creepy is that? Apparently, they all get together every

43

morning at 8:00 to discuss what goes on in here. I wonder if they record when we go to the bathroom too. I have heard that they pay special attention to what we do during recreation.

Known as "forced fun" among the patients, recreation time is almost as hard as small family group, but for different reasons. I had my first experience with it today. It reminds me too much of gym class. We go outside and play games, like basketball or kickball. I used to hate that in school. I was always the last one to be picked for a team. The only difference between gym class and recreation time is that most of the other patients have no athletic ability either.

I hate running around. I feel so stupid. Whenever I run, I can feel my layers of fat flopping up and down. I can only imagine how grotesque I look, but as I mentioned, I am being watched so I need to appear cooperative. Being watched was all I thought about during our kickball game today. I know that Donna, the recreational therapist, attends the 8:00 A.M. meetings, so I did manage to participate, but I hated it.

Tomorrow is Friday, but in here that doesn't mean anything. Fridays in my apartment were the best. I usually shopped for groceries late Thursday night. The store was less crowded then, so there were fewer people to make rude comments about the items in my cart. I spent most of Friday cooking.

When Friday night rolled around, I was set. I would watch my favorite television program, *Beauty and the Beast,* while I was eating dinner. Vincent had someone to love him even though he was ugly. It gave me hope that someday Tim would come around. Then, I watched *Dallas.* I loved to watch J. R. because he was so mean. His character also gave me hope. I wasn't mean. If he was so mean and someone loved him, why couldn't someone love me too?

Fridays in this place would be so different. We are not allowed to watch television. But on Saturday nights, they do let us watch a video. Patients choose it, but counselors can overrule it if they think it isn't suitable for food addicts. I could care less about a movie, though. Watching a movie will only remind me of how safe I felt in my home.

I better do the questions so I can get to bed. I'm emotionally drained. I think being so anxious all of the time exhausts me. Yet, strangely, I have more energy than I have ever had. I can't even believe I'm doing all of the activities on the schedule. I wonder how long I can keep this up.

Question 1 says to reread "The Doctor's Opinion" and discuss the emotional changes I underwent while eating: Under the influence of food, I wasn't able to stop eating. I stuffed all of my feelings down my throat to numb myself from feeling anything. I lost myself because I didn't realize that I have a disease. I blamed myself.

The next question asks about my physical problems from eating. I weigh more than three hundred pounds. It is hard for me to move around and I get tired fast. Because I ate so much, I usually had diarrhea and an upset stomach. My feet always hurt and I couldn't walk far without getting out of breath.

Next, I need to write about how I felt after eating and consider whether I ate to cause these feelings: I felt scared, alone, isolated, angry, upset, hopeless, sneaky, and rejected. No, I ate these foods because I couldn't stop myself from eating. I felt out of control whenever I ate.

The last question asks how my goals for today are

related to what I've been doing since I decided to get help: I want to work on admitting and believing that I have a disease that is not my fault. Before I even knew about food addiction, I blamed myself and hated myself for the way I ate. Now, I can hate the disease instead.

◆ Day 5 ◆

July 7, 1989

I'm exhausted like I've never been. The weirdest thing happened during small family group, and I'm embarrassed, even ashamed. I don't know what came over me or how I could have done such a thing.

The day started out the same as the others here. We had a lecture after breakfast on how to talk about our feelings. I left there confused and went to small family group at 11:00 A.M. just like yesterday. I introduced myself again using my new "affirmation," my positive statement about being likable and lovable.

Beth had another assignment. She had to write an anger letter to her disease. She read about how much she hated the way people looked at her body and how angry she was that strangers criticized her weight.

From as early as I could remember, other kids had always been horrible to me. While Beth was yelling, my head filled with the image of three boys holding their shirts up over their faces so they would not breathe the same air that I did. I had pretended not to notice them, but I was so ashamed.

In fourth grade, I wanted more than anything to be thin like the other kids. I was always the fattest, and most times the tallest, kid in the class. I hated the way they always stared at me like I came from another planet.

When I was ten or twelve years old, I had walked down an aisle of a grocery store to get something while my mother stood in line at the checkout counter. An old man came up to me and looked me directly in the eyes, practically touching my face with his, and said, "You fat slob, why don't you do something about your weight?" I glared at him and then quickly turned away. I felt humiliated for even being out in public.

The more Beth talked about her anger and pain, the more I remembered mine. As she began to sob, the counselor handed her a pillow and told her, "Let it out." She took the pillow, kneeled, and began beating it against the floor again, as she had the other day, but this time she was louder and her anger was more intense.

Listening to her scream, it all came back to me: the picketers who yelled "Baby Killer" and shoved cardboard signs written in blood red in my face as I entered an abortion clinic. How I hated them for forcing me to face what I already knew.

I began rocking my body as I thought about the abortion. I had slept with the father of the baby, Mike, only to prove to myself that someone would actually want me after I had found out that John, my true love, didn't.

When Mike had turned out to be exactly like I was, eating a lot and using the drive-through to avoid embarrassment, I began to hate him for his weakness. We broke up exactly one week before I learned I was pregnant; I was seventeen years old. With no hope of raising a child on my own and fearing that my father would throw me out of the house, I chose to kill my baby.

Rocking back and forth, I thought about the old men walking in front of me waving their signs. As I had entered the clinic, I realized in my heart that they were right. I was about to kill my baby. I had killed my baby. I had killed my baby. I was no better than a murderer, and I hated those men for reminding me of that. I hated them so much.

My body began to shake in anger over the picketers' coldness. Didn't they know that I had no choice?

I hated them and I hated everyone who had ever teased me about my weight. Didn't they know I had tried everything I knew to lose weight? Why did they always have to remind me about my lack of willpower? Did they really think that I didn't know I was fat?

As I continued to shake, the counselor finished helping Beth and then noticed the tears streaming down my cheeks. He handed me the pillow.

"Go ahead. Get it out! You can do it. Think about how much you hate this disease! Take the pillow and kneel on the floor in the center. Go ahead!"

"I can't. . . . My knee. I can't kneel," I yelled, as I continued to rock back and forth.

"That's okay," he said. "Here." He quickly positioned two chairs across from each other in the center of the circle. He motioned for me to sit on one and beat the pillow against the other.

As I thought about how much I hated everyone who had teased me, I began to slam the pillow against the chair. With tears streaming down my cheeks, I beat the pillow and began yelling, "I hate you. I hate you so much. I'm not a baby killer. I hate you so much. I hate you. I hate you. I hate you. I hate you. . . ."

When I was done, I lifted my head and stared directly into the counselor's eyes to see that he was smiling the biggest smile I'd ever seen. And when he told me to look around at everyone else, I saw that they were all still there. Some were smiling, a few were crying, and Patti was sobbing uncontrollably, but when the counselor asked her what was wrong, she refused to answer.

A few minutes later, group was over. I couldn't get out of there fast enough. On the way out, people kept hugging me and telling me how much they understood what I felt. All I felt was stupid for losing control like that. Yet in my room, I realized that I also felt relieved. I was exhausted but also experienced a feeling of peace and serenity. It was like nothing I had ever experienced, and though everyone seemed to act normally toward me at lunch, I still felt strange about what had happened.

The rest of the day, I made it a point to keep to myself as much as possible, though I did talk to Paulette about how embarrassed I was. She told me it was good that I had gotten my anger out. Expressing my feelings, she told me, was the best way to deal with them. Although I didn't really understand everything she had said, I was glad that she was still so nice to me after the spectacle I had made of myself.

Maybe now that I've done so much "anger work," as they call it, they'll let me go early.

Again I have to read "The Doctor's Opinion" section concerning the "phenomenon of craving" and discuss my cravings: I craved love from a significant other most, and nothing else mattered or got in my way to get this love. I tried as hard as I possibly could to control everything so Tim would love me. I craved love from my father and craved attention from most male friends I had. It seemed as if no matter how hard I would try not to, I always craved so much love and attention from men.

I used to crave my bedroom when I lived with my

parents because that was the only place I could binge without anyone seeing me. I craved my soap operas also, because during them I would plan to binge for the afternoon.

Next, I have to write about eating out of control and the feelings I have now about this: I felt as if I had to eat everything in sight when I was out of control. I binged most when I was hurt, lonely, scared, or depressed. Eating helped distract me for a little while. While I ate, I felt euphoric, happy, sneaky, and desperate. After I was done eating, I felt guilty, upset, and depressed.

When I look back on this behavior, I feel grateful to God that I am here among people who love and understand me. I feel anger, embarrassment, and pain when I look back, as well as relief that, for today, I am not bingeing.

Lastly, I have to write about the issues I want to work on today: I wish to work on feeling likable and lovable, and understanding and feeling the anger and depression I have over this disease, and seeing the powerlessness of my disease.

After today, I have no idea what will happen in this place next. I'm terrified to find out.

◆ Day 6 ◆

July 8, 1989

The mornings are the worst. I hate waking up here. The moment I open my eyes is the hardest. While I'm asleep, it's not real, but as soon as I see the tan sheets and comforter filled with bold flowers, I can't deny where I am.

Walking around, going to group, even talking with others over meals (except, of course, gentle breakfast), I'm always looking over my shoulder to see if a counselor or a nurse is watching me. I'm terrified that they'll see me doing something wrong. There is even more talk about everyone on staff watching us and reporting on what we're doing. I believe it.

Last night, I was awakened by the sound of my door opening. Through a fog, I saw a nurse stare at me, then quietly close the door. When I mentioned it to Dawn, who's been here almost three weeks, she said that nurses check on us several times during the night. How creepy to think that a stranger is watching me sleep.

I'm really not sure how much more of this I can take—all of these rules and regulations and no one to talk to about it. I miss my family and friends so much and, of course, Tim. I wonder constantly what he's doing and where he is. I know he was planning to go home to California for a while, but I don't know exactly when.

At night before I fall asleep, I often think about the time we spent together and how much I love him. My favorite was when the four of us—Mark, Tim, Tim's roommate, Jason, and I—went to Boldt Castle in upstate New York. It was a castle on a heart-shaped island that a man was building for his wife. She died before it could be completed.

When I told Tim I thought it was romantic that this man was building a castle for his wife, he said, "Oh, Debbie, I'll build a castle for you." And as he said it, he held his right hand over his heart and got down on one knee. Maybe he was kidding, but either way, I'll never forget that moment.

I keep holding on to how much Tim will love me when I lose all my excess weight. I can already tell that I've lost something, though I don't know how much. They made me get on the scale backward my first full day here, and another patient told me that they weigh us every Monday the same way. We need to concentrate on our recovery, not our weight, the counselors say; the weight is a symptom of food addiction and will take care of itself if we work our recovery program.

Today was a little easier. We got to sleep an extra hour because it's Saturday! And no small family group today— even better. We had a few group meetings in the morning, but nothing intense, then a film about food addiction in the late afternoon.

Right now, most of the other patients are in the lounge watching a movie. After being with these people all day, the last thing I want to do is spend another hour and a half around them. I just want to be alone, but I got a roommate this morning. Terri is from Alabama. She's in her early forties and she's thin. She's a social worker, but she's a food addict too.

I don't think I'm going to like sharing a room. The last time I did, I was six years old and it was with my sister. It's going to be so strange trying to sleep with a stranger in the bed next to mine. With the behavior I've witnessed around here, she could be dangerous. I guess I'll just have to watch what she does closely. They've taken away the only place here where I felt even somewhat safe. Things are getting worse instead of better.

Now the questions. First up, I have to read the first four pages on Step 1 in the book *Twelve Steps and Twelve Traditions* from Alcoholics Anonymous and change all references to alcohol and alcoholism to food and food addiction. The First Step, then, is "We admitted we were powerless over alcohol [food]—that our lives had become unmanageable." For the most part, these pages discuss the same idea I've been hearing around here: I am powerless over food once I take the first bite, just as an alcoholic can't stop drinking after the first drink.

Now, I have to describe how I felt completely defeated and list what I surrendered to be ready to take this First Step. Then I need to discuss my feelings about this Step and the knowledge that I can't control things. I have surrendered my freedom in the outside world, phone calls to my family and friends, completing my degree in August, sleeping late, shopping, and bingeing. I feel scared, anxious, unsure, angry, humiliated, resentful, and relieved.

Lastly, I have to write about how Step 1 motivates me today and what I will do differently. Step 1 means giving up all those garbage messages I've been told since I was little: "Good girls don't get angry. You have no willpower. You always have a choice. There's nothing you can't do if you put your mind to it." These issues have been around all my life. In the past, I blamed myself for these issues. Now, I intend to blame my disease and turn my life over to my Higher Power.

❖ Day 7 ❖

July 9, 1989

Today was one of my hardest days here, for reasons I couldn't have imagined. I had expected today to be easier because I didn't have to go to small family group and I would get an extra hour of sleep.

After breakfast, patients who had been here for seven *full* days were allowed to attend church services. Since I fell half a day short, I couldn't go. As I watched everyone else getting ready, my heart broke. They would be leaving for more than an hour and I was stuck here.

I hadn't been to or wanted to go to church since I was ten years old when my family left our church. The church had insisted that my family pay membership dues for my dead grandfather in order for the pastor to perform burial services.

Today, however, going to church had become what I wanted most. Those allowed to leave put on better clothes and a little more makeup. Paulette's hair had been combed into place and her cheeks blushed slightly. She wore her best clothes.

Watching her walk out the door, I panicked. What if

she didn't come back? How would I ever make it in this place without her? What if the van was in an accident?

I felt as I had so many times in the past, the fat girl left home alone. On the night of my senior prom in high school, I had stayed home and eaten. Even though I had told myself that I didn't want to go, I knew it was a lie. I would have liked nothing more than to get all dressed up and go dancing with a handsome boy on my arm. But I knew from years of experience that fat girls didn't get to do things like that.

A few years later I was invited to go to the prom with a guy I had met on the phone, but that didn't work out either. Chris and I had met each other through a guy I worked with at a grocery store. We talked on the phone for almost a year before I had the courage to let him see how overweight I was. During that period, I had known what it felt like to be a normal girl and I had loved it.

When we finally met, Chris told me that it was better if we remained just friends. He didn't need to say anything. I knew the reason and I was devastated. A few weeks later, I was shocked when he asked me to be his date for his senior prom. I spent weeks looking for just the right dress, one that would fit over my 250-pound body.

As we walked out to his car on prom night and began driving away, Chris informed me that he had forgotten the tickets at home. When I urged him to pick them up, he made up some excuse about not being able to get in once the prom started. Within an hour, I was back home alone in my room crying.

I was interrupted only once by my sister, who had been kind enough to prepare me a dinner plate. I ate that and began eating anything else I could find. I didn't care what happened to me. I felt so foolish and alone. Dying had seemed like an easier way out than living with my humiliation.

Now once again left behind, I was forced to attend a huge group meeting with all of the other remaining patients, including the drug addicts and alcoholics. I hated being with such a big group of people. There must have been sixty or seventy people here. That amazed me, considering that this hospital only handled addictions. All of these people were addicts. At least no counselors were there today.

It was weird to hear drug addicts and alcoholics talk about their feelings. I had always looked down on people who couldn't control their liquor. I thought they were weak and useless. People who did drugs, to me, were the scum of the earth, stupid, and out of control. But when I heard some of them explain how hard it was to stop drinking or using drugs, and the pain from wanting them so badly, I understood.

It's always been like that for me, but with food. Every time I went on a diet, I wanted to lose weight so badly, yet I couldn't stop eating, even just until lunchtime. I would wake up swearing that today was going to be the day I lost weight, only to be breaking the diet by noon.

On one of my last attempts, I woke up full of enthusiasm, then reached for a hot dog only a few hours later. After that, I just kept eating—fried tortillas, popcorn, kielbasa, hamburgers, tomato sandwiches loaded with mayonnaise, and grilled cheese. Most times it didn't matter what the food was, as long as it tasted sweet, crunchy, or creamy.

While I listened to the alcoholics and drug addicts, I remembered things, especially how desperately I wanted to be thin. I would have cut off my right arm for that, yet

I couldn't do something as simple as stop eating foods that were bad for me. It really scared me that I could relate to what these people were saying, especially since I had looked down on them.

Some people here say that food addicts are the same as alcoholics and drug addicts. It's all so confusing. Just because I can understand what they're saying, does that mean we're the same? I really hope not, but from what I read in the two alcoholic books, I feel the same way about food as they do about liquor.

I better get these questions over with. I'm tired of thinking about all of this. The first question says to reread Step 1 in *Twelve Steps and Twelve Traditions* and pick out phrases and tell why they mean something to me.

On page 21, "upon entering A.A. we soon take quite another view of this absolute humiliation." This means a lot to me because yesterday I experienced humiliation when I told everyone that after only five days I was ready to leave, but the absolute part of it came from admitting it to others in a large group. (I'll write more about that tomorrow. I'm too exhausted right now.)

"Admissions of personal powerlessness." I felt this yesterday at that time too. "Spared that last ten or fifteen years of literal hell" means a lot because I have this idea that I haven't suffered enough to recover, but now I know I deserve to recover no matter what mistakes I make.

Next, I have to discuss how my eating affected me and the people in my life: My out-of-control eating made me hate myself. I felt like a failure because I couldn't stop eating. I thought I was worthless and had no willpower. All this made me insecure, full of self-doubt and self-hatred, so when I was alone, I was almost always sad, depressed, and unhappy, but whenever I was with other people, I was happy, up, and positive, always trying to please them.

I used my niceness and up attitude along with my fat to manipulate people into being nice to me or to control them and keep them near me. I thought that if I pleased them enough and captivated them with niceness, they would feel obligated to like me and not leave or hurt me.

My eating caused me to isolate myself while at the same time I lost myself in other people, always trying to help and please them. I never gave anyone, including my family, the chance to know what a likable and lovable person I am just because I am me and not because I could make them happy.

I also never got to know myself, either. I would be rude and resentful when anyone interrupted my eating, and I missed out on having a lot of fun with my sister because I was too fat or tired.

I wish to work on both finding out who I am so I can be myself and believing that I am likable and lovable. I also want to learn to have more fun, if that's possible in a place like this.

July 10, 1989

Something happened a few days ago that I haven't wanted to write about. I've been too embarrassed. I thought that if I ignored it, it would go away, but unfortunately it hasn't. I guess I really need to "get it out," as they say here. I mentioned it yesterday, but, even then, I wasn't willing to face it.

I have never been so humiliated as I was the other day. We did this stupid learning exercise during large family group, and I really messed up. The counselors instructed us to choose a place in a circle according to where we thought we were in our recovery. The outer row was for people who weren't really committed to their recoveries, the middle was for those who were somewhat willing, and the inner was for those who are in recovery.

When we were told to find the area where we belonged, I went and stood in the inner row. People who have been here twice as long as I have still haven't done anger work, so I was sure I belonged in the recovery ring.

This all wouldn't have been so humiliating if Dawn,

my buddy no less, hadn't announced that she didn't think I belonged there. Everyone agreed with her. Even those who had no idea what was going on knew what a horrible mistake I had made.

After group, I started running back to my room to cry, but the head counselor, Marge, stopped me and held me while I cried. "You made a mistake; you are not a mistake," she said. I'm not sure what she meant, but it was kind of nice to know that at least she didn't hate me.

Even today, I really wanted to leave here because of that. Is this humiliation the price I must pay for getting a thin body? I'm not sure I'm willing to do that. Besides, who says that this place is really the answer to my problems? My counselor at school who recommended it? What if I am being brainwashed like in those cults I hear about? Maybe they've already done a good job. Just look at what I've written in this journal so far. My answers are exactly the ones they want me to have. Is that what the key to survival here is—to parrot their answers back to them like in school? I can do that. I'm used to it, but I have to be careful not to believe the things they say, especially if it's going to hurt like it did the other day.

And, if it means getting out of here alive, I can learn to tell them exactly what they want to hear. A counselor told me this morning that my insurance company decides each Monday if it will cover another week's stay. She was happy to report that it had agreed to another seven days. Great. Isn't that wonderful? It makes me sick inside, but I can't let them know. When she told me, I simply smiled as she expected me to.

I feel the same as the woman I heard speak this morning in spirituality group. Her name is Kathy and she scares me. She's very overweight with long, stringy hair, and her voice is harsh and commanding.

In group, everyone was talking about how wonderful God was and how much they loved their Higher Power. Then, all of a sudden, Kathy yelled in her deep voice, "If there's a God, why are there starving children in the world? Why is there such suffering?"

I could hear the anger in her voice and it scared me. But she did bring up a good point. Why does God let people suffer?

Someone else in the group calmly replied that she believed it was "human will" not "God's will" that we suffer. She said that humans get in the way of God's good for others. I'm not sure what to believe, but I do know I'm staying away from Kathy. I'm having enough problems of my own and her yelling like that certainly won't help her get out early.

With my insurance coverage renewed, I have at least another seven days of questions. Here they are. I have to reread "Bill's Story" in the AA book, then write about the things he did that I relate to.

I can relate to the uncontrollable desire and need to eat, then later wondering what's wrong with me. Why couldn't I stop? I can also relate to the powerlessness over eating and over my life. And I can relate to having my disease affect every area of my life. I feel my eating behavior is as serious as Bill's drinking. I couldn't stop eating any more than Bill could stop drinking without this program.

Finally, I need to write about the food issues from my past that I am remembering. I am trying to remember my eating binges. I know there were a lot of them and I ate a lot, but I can't remember many details. I am fearful of remembering the binges because as much as I know I couldn't stop eating, I know more humiliation will come with remembering.

❧ Day 9 ❧

July 11, 1989

This girl read her entire history with food in front of everyone, and then the other patients and counselor told her what they thought or felt about what she had said. While I could really relate, another part of me wondered what the point was. Why did she have to spill her guts in front of everyone? What did it really accomplish?

I guess I'm going to find out soon. On my twenty-first day, I have to read my First Step to the group. I've been trying hard to remember my food history, but I can only seem to recall the last few months before coming here. The rest is a blank. I hardly remember anything from my childhood, and I certainly don't remember all of the things I've eaten during my life and how I felt before, during, and after. To expect that is ridiculous.

I'm hoping that by the time it's my turn, I'll be gone. I'm not sure how, but I really want to get out of here. Yesterday, Michelle tried to leave. She had her bags packed and had called a cab before a group of people talked her out of leaving. It was really emotional for her. I was envious of her courage. To pick up the pay phone and use it before her twenty-one days were up took a lot of nerve. I wish she actually went through with leaving though.

There may be a chance that I'll talk to, even see, my parents before my twenty-one days are over! Next week is "Family Week," when patients' families may come and visit the hospital for a week. A counselor asked me if I wanted my parents to come and I said yes!

They've been so wonderful with sending me cards and letters. Today, the most beautiful bouquet of flowers arrived, filled with roses, daisies, and mounds of baby's breath. The sweet smell was such a nice contrast to the antiseptic odor here. I can only hope they'll come next week.

But now, the questions. First, I have to read the part of "Bill's Story" that talks about hitting bottom and then discuss the bottoms I've hit: I haven't been able to live a normal life since my eating got out of control. I didn't go out with friends much and when I did, I would get angry with them because they were taking me away from food. Getting together with friends usually centered on food. I usually cooked for them or we'd go to dinner.

When I saw the food, I couldn't stay focused on the conversation. I wasn't able to concentrate on my school-work and most of the time was too depressed and full of self-hatred to have energy to do the things I wanted. Because I'm so fat, I wasn't able to do the physical activities I wanted to, such as hiking or horseback riding. I always felt lonely, isolated, and inadequate.

Next, I need to discuss my feelings about some of the things that happened when I hit bottom and whether I can relate to Bill's repeated attempts to become normal. I always tried to eat normally in front of other people, then would go home and binge, or if I were going out to dinner, I would always eat something first. If I were eating at a friend's house, I would eat less than everyone else to prove how "well" I was. I felt lonely, isolated, sneaky, humiliated, and powerless when I tried to pretend I was normal.

I'm starting to realize that maybe the people I hung around with were also food addicts. It seems like most of the times we got together, we ate or talked about food. Most of these people are graduating and will be gone by the time I get back to school.

I feel shocked to realize just now that my friends could possibly be food addicts too. I always tend to think everyone else is so much better than me, and I was proud to have "normal" friends.

◆ Day 10 ◆

July 12, 1989

My father was able to break the rules today. And I loved it! He told the counselor organizing family week, Linda B., that he wouldn't come to Glenbeigh unless he could talk to me first. He told her that he had to be sure I really wanted him and my mother to come.

When Linda told me I could talk to him this morning, I was actually nervous. I'm not sure why. It seemed odd that I was afraid to speak with my own father. I asked Paulette if she would come with me to Linda's office.

As Linda handed me the phone, my hands were shaking and my heart was beating fast. I had no idea what to expect. I haven't spoken to him or my mother in ten days. Grabbing the phone and holding it tightly, I wondered if he thought I was crazy for asking him to drop everything in his busy schedule and fly thousands of miles to come to this torture chamber.

"Hi, Daddy." Those were the only two words I could get out before the tears were rolling down my cheeks.

"Hi, honey. Are you all right? Are they treating you okay there?" As soon as I heard my father's deep voice,

I began to sob uncontrollably as I thought of how horrible this place was and all of the things I'd been through. The pain. The powerlessness. Not getting to leave for church on Sunday. The rigid schedule. These people. . . .

All I wanted was to be at home, safe, with my family. I knew that my daddy would protect me from these awful people if I were home. I wanted to be in my room with its happy orange walls and all of my stuffed animals tucked beneath my worn blanket.

"Deb, are you okay? What are they doing to you there?" I could hear the panic in my father's voice, and it jarred me back to reality.

"Yes, I'm okay," I said still sobbing.

"Are you sure you're all right?"

"I'm fine," I said, remembering the acronym I'd heard for the word *fine*—Fucked-up, Insecure, Neurotic, and Emotional.

"You want me and Mom to come there next week?"

"Yeah, I do," I said between sobs.

"I can only get away for a couple days on such short notice, but we'll be there if that's what you want."

"It is. . . . Thanks." My voice was barely above a whisper through my sobs.

"Okay, honey. We'll see you soon. Karen can't come because of school and work, but Mom and I will be there. Are you sure you're okay?"

"I'm okay, really. It's just good to hear your voice. I have to go now." I began to sob even harder.

"All right, but remember, we love you. And I'm glad I got them to let you talk to me. I'll see you next week."

With my father's job as group vice president of a major grocery-store chain and his hour-long commute each way to his office in New Jersey, he is under a lot of pressure.

My mother has her hands full running the house and taking care of Dad's mom, who lives with them.

My mom underwent two brain surgeries a few years ago to clamp off swollen blood vessels. Since then, I have tried hard to make her life as pleasant as possible. We're lucky she's alive. Well, while I do feel somewhat guilty about dragging my parents here, the gratitude I feel is much stronger.

Maybe their visit will make this last month easier to bear. I can't believe I still have more than a month left. August 14, that's my release date, unless of course they decide to change it. They can keep me here longer than six weeks, and if I leave before they recommend, I'll still be AMA and be responsible for the entire stay, which is something like $25,000.

Because of this, I better do the questions. First I have to reread Step 1 and underline the actions that I can take now. Step 1 is "We admitted we were powerless over alcohol [food]—that our lives had become unmanageable."

Now, I need to describe what rigorous honesty and tolerance have done for me so far at Glenbeigh and decide if they have gotten me to where I am today: Rigorous honesty and tolerance have allowed me to express my feelings, feelings that I never thought I would be able to tell anyone. I feel loved and accepted. These two attributes keep me here. Before I came here, I always felt too ashamed and embarrassed to tell anyone the things I'd done and the way I felt about these actions.

Tolerance before I came here also seemed impossible for me. I always found little things wrong with everyone. Here I tolerate some things I may not accept. And I no longer need to find something wrong with the people here.

Now, I have to discuss how self-centeredness relates to my need for rigorous honesty and tolerance: Self-centeredness caused me to believe that everyone was always laughing at me, that they were always talking about me, and that I was responsible for every bad thing, especially my eating, that ever happened in my life and in the lives of my family and friends. My self-centeredness has sometimes gotten in the way of rigorous honesty and tolerance.

After doing anger work during my short time here, I thought I was different from everyone else, but if I were rigorously honest, I would admit that I wanted to find an easy way out of this place. I am self-centered enough to think that I am not as sick as the other patients here.

I need to be grateful but not proud of the work I've done. I also need to always be honest about my feelings, tolerant of others, but not necessarily accepting and not self-centered. I only need to turn my day over to my Higher Power and be grateful for whatever happens. After all, I made it through yet another day here.

July 13, 1989

Today, I surprised myself. I attended something called
body-image class. I had heard horrible rumors about it.
I kept telling myself that I really wouldn't have to go
through the class. I couldn't face that I would have to do
some of the things I'd heard about. The worst was that
after people went through the class, they had to wear
their shirts tucked into their pants. Today was my turn,
and like everything else here, it was even worse than I
had thought it would be.

Since we are separated by gender in this class, two
other women were with me, one rail thin and the other
chubby. I have no idea what they were thinking putting
the thin one with me.

The three of us walked into the exercise room, where
I have small family group, the room with the mirrors.
Donna, the recreational therapist, told us to stand in a
row facing the mirrors. As I turned to the mirrors, I realized just how difficult it was for me to look at my body
with the layers of fat hanging from it. I have so many
layers of flesh hanging, especially in the middle. There's

at least a six-inch roll of fat pouring over the waist of my tight jeans. How I hated looking at it. It was disgusting. I wanted to run, but I knew that if I did, "consequences" would rule out an early release. I bit the inside of my right cheek and forced myself to pay attention to Donna.

While we were looking at our bodies, Donna told us to describe each other's bodies, beginning at the top and working down. First the chubby woman described the thin one. In this case, they were both lucky. All the chubby one had to say was *thin* about every part of the woman's body. In turn, all the thin one had to hear was *thin*. I would have killed to hear that word about any part of my body. As my turn to be described approached, I again had the urge to run far away. My heart pounded and my eyes filled with tears. Once more, I bit down on the inside of my cheek to stop from crying. The last thing I wanted was for these people to know how much I hated looking at my body. I was sure that Donna would count my weakness against me in some way and I would never be allowed to leave.

As the thin woman began to describe my body, I felt my cheeks redden. She began by saying that my neck was thick and that my arms were a little wide with large wrists. Then, she said my middle area was heavy, my stomach was a little large, and my hips, legs, and calves were big.

It was humiliating to hear her say those things about my body, but it was nothing I hadn't thought of myself. I knew that I was fat, and this thin woman was just verifying it. I hated what she said, but strangely enough I didn't hate her. This was different from all of the times that I had been teased.

This woman spoke softly as she looked my body up and down. She wasn't mean. She was sensitive, even smil-

ing at me when she had finished. She was honest, yet
loving and gentle. I didn't know that the three could
exist together. It was strange for me to experience this.
The only comments I had ever heard about my body
were yelled in disgust and anger.

Then, it was my turn to do the describing. I was surprised to find that it was even harder to describe someone
else's body. Trying to be gentle while still being truthful
was difficult. And, of course, I had to describe the chubby
one. I ended up repeating a lot of what the other woman
said to me, using words like *thick* and *heavy*. Thankfully,
Donna just nodded and smiled when we had finished this
part. I was terrified that she was going to ask us to elaborate on some of our comments.

After that, Donna gave us some string. She said to
take the string and wrap it around our various body parts,
then cut it at that length. We were to use red for what we
didn't like and blue for those parts we accepted. When I
was done, I saw that the only parts I liked were my wrists
and ankles. Finally, we were told to glue the pieces of
string down in circles on large, white pieces of paper and
keep them with us until we leave.

When I looked at how large my circles were, I felt
really sad. The strings representing my hips and thighs
barely fit on the paper. What really struck me, however,
was how much red was on my paper. How sad it is that
I hate my body so much. Yet, this is how I feel.

Donna said it was possible to love your body no matter what its size. That is the most ridiculous statement I
have ever heard. How could I ever love this huge body
with all its layers of fat? That seems impossible.

For the rest of my stay here, I have to wear my shirt
tucked into my pants and look at myself in the mirror for
ten minutes a couple of times a week. And it can't be just

from the chin up like I usually do. I have to look at my entire body and try to like it just the way it is. As I said, I don't see this ever happening, but if it'll get me out of here any sooner, I'll do it.

It really does feel strange to be walking around with my shirt in. Never in my life have I worn it this way. It feels like my stomach is huge and sticking out all over the place. This goes against the rules of being fat, which I have followed my entire life.

- Rule number one: Never wear your shirt tucked in.
- Rule number two: Wear black as often as possible.
- Rule number three: Wear long shirts to cover your rear end.
- Rule number four: Always have perfectly coordinated and pressed clothes to appear perfectly groomed and detract from the size of your body.
- Rule number five: Attempt to attain perfection in all other areas of your life to make up for being such a failure at losing weight.
- Rule number six: Do your best to please as many people as possible so that someone will talk to you when others are around and you won't appear to be a social outcast.

Not only have I lived by these rules for as long as I can remember, but I truly believe them.

Now, I learn that one of my rules is in question here. A few people, even Paulette, told me that I look thinner with my shirt tucked in. Paulette said it shows off my shape instead of hiding it under the big paper sack of a shirt I usually wear. I'm not convinced, but it was nice to hear. I think. I'm not used to getting compliments about my body. It feels strange, even uncomfortable. I just wish everyone would leave me alone so I can do what I need to and get out of here.

Now, the questions. I need to reread the last part of "Bill's Story" and underline the actions that he took to deal with his obsession and then discuss what I am willing to do to be free of my obsession: I am willing to do whatever it takes to have this obsession lifted from me.

Next, I'm supposed to describe how I feel about my obsessive behavior and compare it with Bill's and then tell how it has alienated me from others. Yes, I feel I am as obsessive as Bill. My obsession alienated me from the people I care about because I would stay home to eat, get angry when my eating was interrupted, and fight with my mother over food.

The last question asks what issues I am obsessing about today. Food, the trip I have planned to Disney World, the work here, being here, wanting to go home.

◆ Day 12 ◆

July 14, 1989

I can't believe my luck. I thought I was finally going to escape from this place for a while. I've been locked up here for twelve days and I want to go out already. On some Friday nights, we are allowed to go out to dinner. This is supposed to teach us to weigh and measure in public without worrying about what others think. I was all ready to go, but it turns out that our outing is next week. It's really hard to keep track of the days in this place. Now, I have to wait another seven days to have dinner out. That really stinks! I'm so desperate to go somewhere.

I think that every other patient has gone out, everyone except for me. Some people even get to go to the mall. I can't do that until I've been here for twenty-one days. I can't wait. I love to go shopping. At this point, I'd go to the Laundromat and love it.

For the past twelve days, the only thing I've seen outside of these hospital walls is the damn duck pond and the basketball courts for "forced fun." I've heard of people being allowed to go out on their seventh day, either to dinner or church. But since I started on Monday and it wasn't a full day, I'm in a later cycle.

It will be fourteen days before I am able to attend church, unless of course they take that away from me too. I know that it's only two more days until Sunday, but I really don't know if I can take it. Two days here seems like forever. We have to have every second of our day planned. We even have to schedule what time we'll wash and dry our clothes. There is only one washer and one dryer, so if we miss our time, we wear dirty clothes.

Today, my family counselor gave a lecture about the disease concept and, for the first time, some of it made sense to me. He talked about how some people are born with low levels of certain brain chemicals and overeating triggers a chemical reaction in their systems. He said that food addicts physically crave sugar and flour when they don't get enough because their system is used to maintaining certain levels of brain chemicals. It's like drinking, except this is with food. Food addicts feel calm and tired for a short time after eating sugar and flour. It's because of this that the food addict's body constantly "needs" sugar and flour to keep up these good feelings. Until now, I didn't understand all of the physiological stuff—I've always hated science.

He also said that most of the commercial diets, like Nutri/System and Weight Watchers, put sugar in their prepackaged food. This means that if I am a food addict, I could never succeed on these programs because even small amounts of sugar and flour cause more cravings. If this is really true, then I was just setting myself up for failure all of those times I tried to diet. Although I was eating food that I thought was good for me, I never stopped eating sugar or flour long enough to withdraw from it, so there was no way these diets could have worked. It would be like an alcoholic trying to have just one beer a day—impossible because of the overwhelming physical cravings.

It seems unbelievable that the entire diet industry could be built on such lies. Maybe those diets work for people who want to lose a few pounds. For a food addict, however, it's like throwing money away.

It really makes me mad that more consumers don't know about this. If they did, the diet industry wouldn't be making tons of money off of food addicts who can't control themselves anyway. Talk about repeat business.

When I think of how many times I went to Weight Watchers or Nutri/System, it makes me sick to know that I was doomed before I even started. I can't believe with all of the diet books I've read that I have never even heard of anything like this.

The part I hate to admit is that this information makes sense. Since I've stopped eating sugar and flour, I have not had even *one* craving for any type of food, when before I couldn't go three minutes without one. Yet, while I like the way I feel—clear-headed and alert—I wonder how practical it really is. How long after I leave this place can I continue to stay away from sugar and flour? And, even harder, how can I weigh and measure my food once I leave?

Right now, I'm more concerned about having been taken advantage of. The lecturer said that people pay more than thirty billion dollars each year to lose weight and not even 5 percent of them keep it off for longer than five years. If all of this is true, hasn't anyone thought about what's wrong with the diets on the market?

Time for the questions. It says to read chapter 2 in the AA book titled "There Is a Solution," and write about our "common solution" to problems before coming here. I didn't really understand the whole thing. But I did get that once the alcoholic stops drinking, there's more work to do, such as self-searching and spiritual assistance.

Bingeing was our common solution. No, I don't believe this can work for me again. Being at Glenbeigh has changed my mind. Even though I hate it here, I have never felt more loved or less alone.

Letting food go is only the beginning of recovery. There's so much anger and frustration to work out and so much more to learn about myself and the kind of person I am, what I want and what I don't want. I need to establish a better relationship with my Higher Power too.

Now, I need to make a list of things I can do to help my recovery:

Confront patients with their actions.
Listen to them.
Support them.
Love them.

Finally, I need to discuss the issues these questions bring up. They bring me closer to accepting that I do have a disease. It makes me hate the disease and hate that I can *never* eat just one of anything.

◆ Day 13 ◆

July 15, 1989

This is my second Saturday here and I hate it. It seems like I should get time off for good behavior or something. Don't prisoners get that? The weekends used to be my favorite part of the week.

In my individual session, we were talking about my parents coming here next week. Linda P. asked me what I was going to talk to them about. When I said I didn't have any idea, she asked whether I should tell my father about my abortion.

The minute she suggested that, my heart stopped beating. How could I ever do that? What would he think of me? I hated myself so much; I couldn't take it if he ended up hating me too. I didn't say much after that. But before I left, Linda said, "We're only as sick as our secrets."

If that's the case, I may want to remain sick. Even thinking of telling my father something like that completely overwhelms me. He's Catholic, though he doesn't go to church, and I'm sure he would hate me for what I've done. I just can't think about that right now. Hopefully,

Linda will forget about this by the time my parents come on Monday.

Linda also gave me an assignment to read during small family group. She told me to list ten situations in which I was depressed. Here goes:

1. I was depressed when I had an abortion. It made me feel like a killer. I felt guilty, angry, overwhelmed, and demoralized.
2. I was depressed when the guy I am in love with (Tim) told me that he didn't have a need to talk to me when I had believed he cared. I felt abandoned, isolated, angry, alone, betrayed, spiteful, and embarrassed.
3. I was depressed when my mom had surgery. I felt alone, hopeless, confused, frightened, and angry.
4. I was depressed when I used to go to work on Saturdays. I would be the only one there, so I would binge while I worked. I felt angry, resentful, guilty, and sneaky.
5. I was depressed whenever I felt as if my father loved my sister more than me. I felt abandoned, angry, unloved, and jealous.
6. I was depressed when my friends in Syracuse would have other plans like a date and I would stay home alone and binge on weekend nights. I felt betrayed, angry, hopeless, unloved, and alone.
7. I was depressed when my bedroom at home got flooded with water and I lost my favorite stuffed animal. I felt sad, sickened, angry, and shocked.

8. I was depressed when my friend moved to California. I felt sad, downhearted, tearful, lonely, and angry.

9. I was depressed when I had to leave Syracuse before graduating so that I was still covered under my father's insurance; when I get back, my friends won't be there. I felt alone, panicky, scared, uncertain, anxious, and angry.

10. I was depressed when I listened to everyone's stories at my first support group meeting. I felt awkward, uncomfortable, unsure, relieved, and angry.

I'll have to read this soon. I can't think about that. I just better do the questions and get to sleep. That way this day will be over with already. Maybe I can dream myself into happiness.

To begin, I have to read page 20 in the Big Book about being recovered. According to the reading, being recovered means not eating compulsively to deal with problems, not always feeling lonely or scared, and, most of all, learning and finding out who I am and what I want or don't want.

While I was compulsively eating, I was always lonely, scared, smiling at everyone I met, and afraid to get angry. Being abstinent, I do get angry and I don't feel desperately alone like I once did. I'm aware just how much I smile and I have tons more energy.

Before I came here, my family and friends would say I was always happy, didn't have any problems, never had enough energy, and was lazy with no willpower.

Now, I have to write about the idea that food addiction is a problem of the mind and discuss whether that

is more serious than the physical aspects of the disease:
I feel it is emotional because there is so much anger and
other feelings I need to deal with, and physical because
I am so fat.

Finally, I'm to write about the issues I want to work on:
Staying here. I want to go home very bad. It's important
that I work through these issues because this is where I
need to be; I've done some good work here.

◆ Day 14 ◆

July 16, 1989

I was allowed to leave this place! At 9:45 A.M., I boarded a large, white van with twelve other patients. I had never even seen a van that big. I was worried about being able to fit in my seat. Since the others had already gone before, they knew enough to take the front two rows of seats first, so I had to climb over the tire and squeeze into the last row. I was so afraid of getting stuck there.

On the bumpy ride to the church, I had no idea what to expect. The last time I attended any kind of church service, it was in the Russian Orthodox faith. I had never even heard of the Unity Church. I only chose this church because everyone else said it was wonderful.

But none of that mattered as I sat in the van watching the lush, green palm trees gently blowing in the wind. It felt so wonderful to finally be free of that awful place. The sticky humidity in the van hardly seemed to matter as I watched the small birds flying from tree to tree. How I envied their freedom.

The fifteen-minute ride through city streets reminded me of the safety I had always felt in my father's car on long family rides. Sitting in the backseat of his luxury car, I would watch the woodsy New England scenery on the half-hour ride to my grandmother's house. I would dream both of the luscious treats I knew would be waiting for me and of the prince I knew would someday save me from myself.

Today, I was simply a prisoner on furlough for a few hours. Arriving at the church, I was surprised to see a sign designating the building as one for Seventh-Day Evangelists.

"Unity uses it for services on Sunday," Michelle whispered to me.

Walking in a protected group, we chose seats several pews from the front in the small church. Glancing around, I noticed several families with children. I wondered if they knew how lucky they were. I was especially envious of the women I saw. Each one had a man who had committed his life to her and, together, they were raising a family and loving each other. What else mattered?

A single tear ran down my cheek as I remembered Tim's last words to me: "We aren't the kind of friends who call each other every day. My life is fine with you and fine without you. I have my computer and baseball cards. I don't need human companionship."

Even now, I still don't believe Tim's words. We had spent too much time together and had too much fun for him to mean those things. Yet, I couldn't explain why he had been so cruel. Mark and I had talked for hours about it, only to conclude that Tim was distant in intimate relationships. But I never told Mark that I was sure Tim would have loved me if I were thin.

Lost in thoughts about Tim, I had missed the beginning of the service. A frail older man and middle-aged woman were talking about how God wants only the best for us, that He will protect us and shelter us from harm. What struck me most about these two people—who I later discovered were father and daughter—was the calmness in their voices. They seemed to believe in what they were saying. It was almost as if they were surrounded by a yellow, healing light.

The longer I listened to them, the calmer I felt. Their soothing words talked of a love greater than any other that would always be there to help us. Then we rose to sing together. And though I had never been much for singing—I always felt I couldn't carry a tune—I raised my voice high, reading the words from the songbook. I was surprised by how joyous I felt.

After a "Prayer of Protection," the minister invited everyone downstairs for cake and coffee. I only wished I had the freedom to go, I thought as I followed the others back to the van to begin the much-too-short ride back to my prison.

I know that I'll go again next Sunday, and it won't be only as an escape. I enjoyed listening to those people, and somehow I came away believing that things would work out for me, that some way I would survive the next month here, and that this God those people spoke of would protect me from any harm I may face here. I certainly hope that He watches over me tomorrow when my parents arrive. I am actually a little nervous about seeing them.

It's nearing lights out, so I had better get to the questions. Step Two in the AA book reads, "Came to believe that a Power greater than ourselves could restore us to sanity." And, though I don't understand the entire chapter, it talks about letting God work His will, rather than dictating our wants to Him.

The first question asks me to consider how my Higher

Power is present in my life today. I believe that my Higher Power is always with me. I have begun praying morning and night for the strength and knowledge to do His will. Yes, I really understand the concept of a Higher Power. He is God and He loves me no matter what and I place my life in His hands.

Next, I need to discuss my lingering feelings that somehow I will be able to "beat" the game of my addiction. I feel real scared but at the same time peaceful because of my Higher Power. Sometimes I still think that I don't need this place, that I can do it myself, but every time I hear people talk about their food histories, I see the powerlessness so clearly and realize how unmanageable my life is.

I wish to work on turning my life over completely to my Higher Power without the lingering thoughts that maybe I should pray for this or that.

◆ Day 15 ◆

July 17, 1989

They're here! After breakfast my parents finally arrived
for the first day of family week. I ran up and gave them
both a big hug. While I was eating breakfast, they were
going through an orientation. My father said they were
asked to sign a paper promising not to bring any food
into the hospital and agreeing to follow the food plan,
including weighing and measuring their food.

My parents crossed out the part about eating the way
I do. Can't say I blame them. After the orientation, my
parents went to a lecture about food addiction and I went
to one about spirituality. It felt weird that they were in
the same building while I was going through my day.

It was even stranger to weigh and measure my food
in front of them at lunch. I felt so clumsy. It was like my
first day all over. I kept dropping my food and had to use
my fingers a lot. But my parents were great about it. They
said I looked good, so I guess I really must have lost some
weight. Maybe these people here aren't just being nice.

This afternoon the counselor divided us into groups,
including our families, then instructed our families to

make a list of things they wanted from us and us list what we wanted from them. After that, we had to share our lists in front of everyone. What really surprised me was that my mom and dad said they wanted me to tell them more often how I feel. I really didn't know that I wasn't.

The really strange part, though, was that I had also said I wanted the same thing from them; I wanted to know how they were feeling. It never crossed my mind to talk to them about how unhappy I was. I just always thought they knew, that I didn't have to say anything.

The rest of the day was calm compared with that. We had dinner, went to another, less formal group meeting with everyone, then watched a film about food addiction. They left a little after 8:00 P.M. for their hotel. I really didn't want them to go, but I was exhausted by all of it too. Yet, of course, I still had homework to do.

I spent my hour of free time before snack working on my First Step. It's really a hard thing to do: write down my entire life history with food. Much of my childhood, even into my early teen years, I still don't remember.

The earliest sign of my food addiction is from a story I've heard many times about when I was four or five years old. My mother says that on the forty-minute ride from my grandparents' house, she had to buy me an ice-cream cone or I would cry incessantly.

Before I came here, I considered this one of those cute stories parents like to tell. But since hearing everyone else's First Steps, I realize how early my problem began. As far back as I can remember, I've always overeaten, tried to diet, and hated myself when I failed. It was a horrible, vicious cycle filled with shame.

I spent so much of my life—before, during, and after my teenage years—trying to control what I ate and feeling ashamed because I couldn't. And now, years later, I find out that none of it was my fault. They constantly say around here that I have a disease that affects my brain chemicals, in the same way a person with cancer suffers from a sickness of the body cells.

Sometimes it's hard to really understand that, but thinking of it like cancer helps. A person who has cancer isn't to blame for his or her situation, so why should I be? Yet the other side of it, as the counselors here say, is that I am responsible for my recovery. Just as a cancer patient has to get to chemotherapy, a food addict needs to do certain things to stay healthy, such as weighing and measuring food.

Oh, speaking of the food I'm eating, it's amazing to me that I'm actually enjoying some of it. Breakfast is my favorite meal because I only have to bring my cups, no measuring spoons or scales, and the cup of blueberries and strawberries mixed with a half-cup of plain, nonfat yogurt with a sweetener is absolutely delicious. It's amazing how much a cup of fruit really is. Then, when you add cereal with skim milk, the meal is wonderful.

At first, the skim milk tasted so watery and disgusting, I had to force myself to drink it, but now I don't even notice. Just like with the vegetables. It's getting easier to eat plain, steamed vegetables. My favorite meals have been the two when the chef measured out everything but the salad and combined it into individual casseroles. I liked not having to weigh and measure before eating, but I'm even getting used to that.

And on top of it all, even without my parents saying anything today, I feel like I am losing weight. My jeans are getting looser. I have no idea how much I've lost, but other people are telling me that I'm looking good. I mean, how can they really tell? It's only been two weeks. Do people really start to look better that quickly?

July 18, 1989

If it's true that you're only as sick as your secrets, today I am a little less sick. I told my father something that I should have six years ago. This morning when I met with Linda, once again she asked me if there was anything I wanted to discuss with my parents. There wasn't anything big that I wanted to talk to my mom about. Over the years, we have been pretty close, talking about things like my latest love, my writing career, and my friends. The only thing we never talked about was how much pain I was in because of my weight and overeating, but I always thought she knew. Many times we would even begin diets together, though I always pretended I did it for her.

My father, however, was a different story. I never found it easy to talk with him about the really important things. He is over six feet tall, and I often found myself tongue-tied around him. I respected him so much that I felt unworthy of his time.

Since the age of sixteen, when he began bagging groceries, my father has advanced himself in his career. With an incredible amount of work, he has finally become group vice president of the country's largest grocery-store region—New York City, New Jersey, Long Island, and parts of Pennsylvania and Connecticut. Each day, he commutes an hour and fifteen minutes to his office in New Jersey, putting in twelve- to fourteen-hour days.

I always felt I had to be perfect to live up to his examples of dedication and drive. Yet I have never felt capable of doing that. In school, I did just enough to get by, always opting instead to eat and watch television. I certainly didn't think anyone would recognize me as the daughter of this incredibly successful man.

Before I came here, I had never even considered telling him about my abortion. Part of it was my pride and desire to prove him wrong about the man who got me pregnant; my father had hated him from the instant he met him. The other part was an overwhelming fear that he wouldn't love me anymore.

When Linda asked if I needed to discuss anything with my parents, I knew she meant telling my father about the abortion. While I didn't want to relive that horrible pain, my drive to maintain my recovery was strong. And that saying about only being as sick as your secrets rang through my head as I blurted out to Linda that I should tell my father about the abortion.

Looking me right in the eyes, she asked me why I hadn't. I told her that I was afraid of losing his love. Ending the session once again by reminding me that I am only as sick as those things I choose to hide, she mentioned the family meeting with her this afternoon. With my parents leaving tomorrow, would there be a better time?

For the rest of the morning and through lunch, I could hardly concentrate on anything else as an overwhelming fear rose up in me. My stomach ached, my heart pounded wildly, and my hands shook as I tried to plan what I would say to my father. As I inhaled my lunch, never even tasting it, I studied the clock. Our meeting was scheduled for fifteen minutes after lunch and I was no more prepared than I had been at 10:00 A.M.

Those fifteen minutes were a blur as I went through my thrice-daily chore of washing my measuring instruments. Before I knew it, the three of us were sitting in Linda's small office and she was asking me if there was anything I wanted to tell my parents.

As my body shook and my heart pounded loudly, I looked my father directly in the eyes and began to cry. How could I ever tell this great man what a horrible mistake I had made? Tears ran down my cheeks. I quickly looked away, drying my cheeks before I took a deep breath and began to speak.

"Dad . . . uh . . . Oh, Daddy. There's something I never told you." I looked at my father sitting there, leaning slightly forward and full of love in his eyes, and I began to sob. "I was afraid, so afraid. . . . I thought you wouldn't love me anymore if you knew."

I couldn't seem to go on until I glanced at Linda. I could feel her presence, willing me to continue, presiding over the scene.

Taking a deep breath and drying my eyes, I said, "When I was seventeen, I had an abortion. . . ."

My father's face was expressionless. I desperately wanted to know what he was thinking. Did he still love me? Was I going to be thrown out of his life? Had I destroyed our relationship forever?

Looking at my father, Linda asked him how he felt.

"It doesn't matter, but what I do feel is hurt that she—"

"Talk to Debbie," Linda instructed my father.

"That you thought I wouldn't love you anymore," my father's voice was soft as he looked in my eyes. "I thought you knew that your mother and I would love you no matter what."

I could control my tears no longer and sobbed. These were the words that I always hoped to hear from him but could never ask for. That this great man could love me so unconditionally was more than I had ever imagined possible.

"Debbie, is there anything you need?" Linda asked.

"I don't know . . . I'm not sure. . . ." I quickly wiped my face once again.

"Maybe a hug or something?" Linda suggested.

"Yeah, I could use a hug."

And before I could even stand up, my father was on his feet, holding me in his arms and telling me that he loved me. For the first time, I looked at my mother and saw tears in her eyes, and I reached for her too.

For the rest of the day, as we watched films and listened to discussions, I felt so special and loved. My parents had come all this way to help me. I couldn't have asked for anything more. If I had needed proof of their love, I found it these past two days in the most challenging hours of my life.

I felt light and free, even a little bit healthier. My deepest secret was out. My father knew of my greatest mistake and he still loved me. Equally as wonderful was that he hadn't asked me any questions. It hadn't been necessary for me to tell him who the father was and there were none of the "I told you so's" that I had expected. Thank God for getting me through this.

◆ Day 17 ◆

July 19, 1989

It's amazing what my parents have learned in such a short time. Before they left this morning, we talked a little about Glenbeigh and the program. They seemed to understand the addiction part of everything and even said being here was good for me.

It's funny because that gave me mixed feelings. Part of me is glad they are so supportive of what I'm doing, but the other part wanted them to hate it here. I even hoped they'd take me home with them because they were so suspicious of what was going on. But I'm still here. They get to go back to their lives while I'm locked up in this place.

After they left, I felt sad and lonely being back in the same old routine. I won't be able to talk to them again for four more days. I won't even know if they got home safely. What if their plane crashes? How will I find out? I can't call anyone until Sunday, July 23, when I get to make two fifteen-minute phone calls, unless of course I mess up and lose a day. Every time I pass the two pay phones in the hall, I glance at the sign-up sheets. On

Sunday I'll finally be able to schedule times to make phone calls myself.

Then my problem is whom to call. I know my first call will be to my parents, but what about the second? I want to talk to my sister, but I also want to talk to Mark—we used to see each other every day—and there's my friend Wendy too. I miss them all.

The sad truth is that I really want to talk to Tim. I keep thinking that he really didn't mean what he said to me about his life being fine with me and fine without me. Maybe he was just having a bad day.

Yet as much as I want to talk to Tim, I know I can't call him. I'm afraid he would just hang up on me, or worse, tell me never to speak to him again. At least this way, I can wonder if he really meant what he said instead of knowing for sure.

I worked on my First Step tonight and I discovered something more about my relationships. It seems that I buy things for people to get them to like me. When I first started writing my food history and thinking about this, I told myself that I was just being a nice person. I'm starting to realize that I took my niceness too far.

I bought Tim a lot of gifts for Christmas, spending at least $100. Yet I was careful not to buy him anything really expensive looking, though the price didn't matter to me. It would have been nice if he had gotten me a Christmas present, but pleasing Tim is what really mattered to me. I loved watching his face light up when he opened the gifts, and when he told me I was the nicest person he'd ever met. I just don't understand why he said those awful things to me just a few months later.

For my questions tonight, I have to write about my design for living as it's described in chapter 2 of the AA book and discuss whether the directions outlined by Alcoholics Anonymous will work for me. My design for living is to realize that I can't control people, places, things, or changes. All this is in the hands of God and whatever happens is what's supposed to.

I've seen recovery in others. Yes, I believe the directions are for me. I only pray that I am able to make it through. I'm scared to death about making drastic changes. I feel scared, anxious, angry, and hopeful.

July 20, 1989

Tracy, who has been here nearly three weeks, tried to leave. I'm not sure what lead up to it, probably something in group, but when I saw her, she was red faced, crying hysterically, saying that she couldn't stay here even one more second.

She seemed fine earlier. I had even sat with her at breakfast. During family group later in the morning, she cried a little about her relationship with her father.

In this place, it's an abnormal day if someone doesn't cry or scream. It's amazing how quickly you get used to seeing so much emotion. It's so much different now than it was in the beginning, when all these people had to do was look at me and I cried.

When I came back from painting a heart-shaped dish in ceramics, part of our "forced fun," I saw Tracy near the phone at the nurses' station. She was sobbing and her face was red. She was yelling at a nurse that she wanted to go home. As she screamed and cried at the same time, her mouth was open so wide that it looked as if the elastic bands in her braces were going to snap.

A small group gathered, and several of the patients tried to talk Tracy out of leaving, while one nurse frantically pushed buttons on her telephone. Within seconds, my counselor, Linda, arrived and gently told Tracy that she would be only hurting herself if she left this far into her treatment, that things weren't always going to seem this bad.

Tracy didn't even seem to hear Linda's soothing words. She was crying so hard that all she seemed to be aware of was her own pain, until Linda motioned for us to gather around Tracy.

"What you're seeing here is the disease in action!" Linda yelled as she motioned for us to move still closer to Tracy.

"Tracy, I feel sad that you're leaving. I'll miss you," one girl cried, as she tried to hug Tracy, only to be pushed roughly away.

"Try to hang in there, Tracy. It'll be okay. You'll get through this," an older woman practically begged Tracy to stay.

Then it was my turn. Though I really never felt close to Tracy, I thought it was my responsibility to say something, anything, to urge her to stay. Yet, I had no idea what it should be. If anyone in this place was the exact opposite of me, it was Tracy.

Thin and pretty, Tracy was one of those girls who had been involved in everything during high school and college. She was a former cheerleader and a student who regularly made straight A's. The flaw in an otherwise-perfect life was her bulimia. With that and her self-hatred, Tracy constantly felt sorry for herself.

There was nothing I hated more than self-pity. I had lived with these feelings for several years after my grandmother moved in, and her constant health problems had only pushed me away from her. Every time I saw Tracy, I was reminded of my grandmother's depression that I had lived with for so long. My parents had taught me to take action, to go after what I wanted, instead of sitting there feeling sorry for myself. My grandmother's depression only reminded me of how miserable I truly was.

Yet I admired Tracy's courage as she blatantly ignored everyone around her and picked up the phone to call her parents. When her parents refused to let her come home, again Tracy willfully grabbed the phone and called for a taxi.

I was afraid for her too. At twenty-two years old, she had been hospitalized several times for bulimia, once nearly dying because of her emaciated condition. And though she had gained weight since then, she still might suffer permanent damage to her digestive system and lose her teeth.

Suddenly, I understood how much her life depended on staying here. Though she hadn't made major progress in accepting her disease, Tracy had stayed on the food plan and refrained from purging for nearly three weeks. If she left now, she would probably die within a year or two. I turned toward Tracy as she hung up the phone and continued to cry hysterically.

"Tracy, I feel scared. I'm afraid of what will happen to you if you leave here." My voice was barely a whisper, as I was shocked to feel the moisture from tears across my cheeks.

I impressed myself by stating my feelings the way they had told us to. The "I feel _____" method meant starting by saying how we felt instead of what the other person did. I felt sort of strange talking like that, but everyone else here did.

I studied Tracy for any acknowledgment. She looked

directly in my eyes for a moment, before pushing past me and lugging her empty suitcases through the group toward her room to pack.

She was about to turn the corner to her room when my buddy, Dawn, her dark eyes full of emotion, stepped in front of Tracy, blocking her way.

"This doesn't feel right to me," Dawn firmly held Tracy's gaze as she spoke sternly. "I feel angry."

Everyone froze. Even the nurse who had been on the phone stopped and listened.

"I think she's faking it. I don't think she's really going to leave. She just wants attention." Dawn spoke evenly and gently, as Tracy glared at her.

"She's right. Oh, God, she's right." Tracy's words were lost beneath her sobs. "My parents know that I have to stay here. . . ."

Dawn wrapped her arms around Tracy, held her, and led her back to her room. Linda followed. The public show was over.

Later, after dinner, Tracy thanked me for what I had said. And, as I smiled at her, a small part of me couldn't help but think how weak she was. Tracy had had her chance to escape and she had thrown it away.

◆ Day 19 ◆

July 21, 1989

Today I finally got to go out to dinner with the others. While it was great to get out of this place again, it was totally embarrassing to weigh and measure my food in public. It seemed like everyone in the restaurant was looking at me as I pushed my broccoli into my cup. And what I mess I made! I had to ask for an extra plate to put the leftover steak on and send the waitress back for more vegetables so my cup would be full.

The only thing that made dinner bearable was that thirty or so other people were weighing and measuring too. I chose a booth near the back of our section so I could blend into the crowd. I didn't want someone to stare at me or, even worse, to say something.

I sat with three others, including Tracy. I should have known how upbeat the conversation would be. A lot of it was just the usual stuff about hating Glenbeigh and bitching about the counselors and the assignments. Then the topic turned to working the program in the "real world." Tracy talked about other people's reactions to the program and said no way did she ever want to weigh and measure her food on a date. The other two people in our booth were married and her comment didn't seem to affect them.

I repeated what I had heard here about not wanting to be with someone who wouldn't accept me for who I am, but her words have haunted me since. I tried to picture Tim's reaction if we were out to dinner and I pulled out measuring cups, spoons, and a scale. I knew he'd probably be horrified and that we'd probably never go out to dinner again.

I thought about graduation dinners, celebrations for new jobs, business lunches, birthday dinners, wedding receptions, even holiday meals. How on earth would I ever be able to face this? From what they tell me here, the food plan I'm on now, with the exception of small adjustments for maintenance, will remain the same forever.

They say "one day at a time," but I don't know how that's possible. I mean, weighing and measuring all the time without exception just doesn't seem realistic. I could just imagine what my future boss would say if we went out to lunch and I whipped out my measuring instruments. I'd probably be fired on the spot.

It just all seems so hopeless, yet people here have done this for many years. My counselor, Linda, has been abstinent for something like five years, and this other woman Lisa has two years of following the food plan. Still, I wonder if I'm someone who can do this for any length of time.

In here, there's really no challenge. It's not like I'm going to overeat or binge with all of these people watching. Maybe realizing how sheltered I am in here is part of what bothered me when we went out for dinner. As we walked through the mall to the restaurant tonight, the smell of popcorn was overwhelming.

I had no idea how much something as innocent as the smell of one of my favorite foods would affect me. I wanted to run to the popcorn machine and shove handfuls into my mouth, and that scared me more than anything here ever has.

For the past nineteen days, I have felt better physically than ever before. I've done things that I never imagined: group exercises, getting up at 6:00 A.M. for five consecutive days, and walking almost daily, and it's been wonderful. I really don't want to lose the things I've gained, and I know they're all because of the way I'm eating now.

It really is scary, and I have no idea how things will work out. That passage I've been reading every night says a Higher Power, or God, is supposed to take care of me. I'm not sure I believe that, but it's a nice thought that will at least help me survive this place. I hope.

Time for the questions. To begin, I have to discuss being a devout, fat, and serene person and relate it to my life. I have always been devoted to my image as the happy, people-pleasing, fat, serene, always-smiling person on the outside, while I was hurting deeply on the inside. It's insane to pretend to be so sweet when I'm really pissed off.

Next, I have to write about how material success is connected to a Higher Power. I have everything materially that I could ever ask for, so it makes it harder to believe there is no God at all. There's no way I could have what I have without a Higher Power watching over me.

Now, I have to discuss sanity and insanity, rational and irrational, spiritual and religious, and describe how they are different. Sanity is living abstinently; insanity is bingeing. Rational is expressing my feelings as I feel them; irrational is pretending to always be happy and sweet. I am praying to have sanity and to be rational and spiritual. Spiritual is knowing God is always with me; religious is worshipping God and fearing Him.

➤ Day 20 ➤

July 22, 1989

I really appreciated the extra hour of sleep this morning. I don't think I've ever felt this emotionally and physically exhausted. Today, in journal group this new girl, Patti, talked about how awful the stress of being here is. As she talked, she cried and I felt really sad for her, but even more so for myself.

Being here is harder than I had ever imagined. The constant fear of being caught doing something wrong is so overwhelming. Some days I try not to even talk too much, yet if I don't share enough of myself, then I'm seen as not working hard enough. It's just like when I used to overeat. I was always looking over my shoulder to make sure no one was watching me eat. I thought this place was supposed to be about getting better, but I feel so horrible.

The thing I'm most afraid of is the assignments. First, there are the written assignments, usually a list of consequences of the disease or ten secrets about our lives. While these assignments are hard, they don't even compare to the other kinds. I'm not even sure what to call these assignments; they involve taking or not taking some action.

For instance, the counselors decided that Cheryl dresses too perfectly, so they put her on "mismatch assignment." She has to wear different colors of socks and of shoes and a plaid shirt with striped pants. Diana, who has problems with feeling feminine, got "dress-up assignment." She has to wear a dress all day long, except during recreation.

Patients like Tammy, who try to take care of others, are put on "no caretaking," while those who use humor or smiles to hide their feelings are given a "no joke, no smile" order. And, if someone is too neat, they are put on "slob assignment," where they can't make their bed or clean up their rooms.

Other assignments are designed to take away patients' masks. For example, those who hide behind makeup are put on the "no makeup assignment," while people who use tears or whining to hide their feelings are forbidden from doing either. And to make sure that everyone else knows what assignments people are on, assignees are required to wear cardboard signs around their necks noting their orders.

Wearing a sign proclaiming your weaknesses must be absolutely humiliating. How stupid. I really, really hope that never happens to me. I'm trying to do exactly what they say to avoid something so embarrassing.

Today, I was moved into a different room, one in the chemical dependency (CD) unit. It seems that there are more people here than they can handle on the FAP unit, so some had to be moved off. At first, I was really angry. Why should I be put in with the alcoholics and drug addicts? I don't even know any of them and fraternizing with them is forbidden. I think the counselors are afraid that FAP patients will fall in love with CD patients and forget about their programs.

I was telling this woman I really like, Ramona, that I was angry about being moved, and she said they only put people in the CD unit whom they think they can trust. That must mean I'm doing something right, even if it does suck to have a new roommate, who, by the way, is a nun! Her name is Ellen and she's a Roman Catholic nun! It's pretty weird if I think about it, but most times I forget. I mean, it's not like she wears her uniform here, so she looks like everyone else. The funny thing is that she's a food addict like I am.

I really need to do the questions and go over my First Step one more time. I finished writing my Step the night before last; now I have to read it again. I'm scheduled to share it tomorrow afternoon at 2:00. I'm trying not to think about it, because if I do, I think I'll go crazy. I can't even imagine telling everyone my deepest secrets about food and eating. I hope I can make it through. If not, they may keep me here longer and that would surely kill me.

The questions say to read chapter 3 in the Big Book, then comment on the phrases I can relate to: "There is no such thing as making a normal drinker [eater] out of an alcoholic [food addict]." I always need to remember this, because I still think I can be cured.

"Pitiful and incomprehensible demoralization." This is what I feel I've gone through as a result of this disease.

"Once an alcoholic [food addict], always an alcoholic [food addict]." I can never forget this.

Now, I need to write about whether I can diagnose myself and whether I classify myself as a "problem eater or controlled eater." I am starting to realize that I can no longer say that I'm not a food addict. I know I am not able to control my eating and I hate to admit it. I am a food addict (problem eater) because I always want to eat everything in sight.

Finally, I need to discuss what issues this raises in my life and if I understand more than I did yesterday. Accepting the concept of a disease and just how powerless I am over food, and everything else for that matter, is what I need to work on. Yes, I am starting to understand that there's no way I can *ever* control anything having to do with choosing food on my own. I am not capable of making a decision about food amounts either.

◆ *Day 21* ◆

July 23, 1989

I woke up terrified. I knew that I was about to tell these
people, practically complete strangers, my life story with
food. Luckily, I was able to attend church in the morning
and the sermon really helped. The minister said something about God taking care of everything exactly the
way it is best for everyone.

Throughout the day, I thought about how some people
believe that things are predetermined. The more I clung
to that, the easier it was to survive the morning. If things
are already decided, then why should I worry about my
First Step? God already has decided whether my counselor, Linda, is going to "accept" my First Step.

The entire morning I could cling to the thought of a
Divine plan, but at lunch it hit me. In little more than
an hour, I was going to disclose my deepest, most hidden
secrets—all of the embarrassing things I've done with
food and the things I'm most ashamed of.

What would these people think? Even more, what
would they say when I was done reading? That's the way
First Steps work—you read everything first without being

interrupted by anyone, except maybe your counselor, then only if you're doing something wrong. After you finish reading, everyone gets to comment.

To make it easier, I asked Paulette to sit next to me. Out of everyone here, she's the one I feel closest to. Unlike a lot of the others, she's gentle and calm. She doesn't yell a lot, yet still gets her point across. Then I asked Ellen, my new roommate, to sit on the other side of me. She is strong and I needed that strength to get through this.

At exactly 2:00 P.M. the doors to the family room were closed and everyone was seated in a large circle around me. Luckily for me, because it's Sunday, some people were on the mall outing, so only about twenty people were there instead of the usual thirty. We all joined hands.

"God, grant me the serenity to accept the things I cannot change, the courage to change the things I can, and the wisdom to know the difference." Our voices chanted in unison as my body shook. My hands were cold and my heart pounded harder than I had thought it could. I reached for my notebook.

As I began to speak, the only other sound was the purring of the refrigerator used to store patients' extra sodas. Taking a deep breath, I concentrated on that sound. It was almost comforting.

"My name is Debbie. I'm a food addict and I'm likable, lovable, and capable. I feel nervous, scared, and anxious."

"Hi, Debbie."

I looked at Linda. She nodded. It was time to begin reading.

"I remember my mom telling me that when I was five years old, she had to stop during the forty-minute ride from my grandmother's to buy me an ice cream. This would ensure that I would be good on the way home."

I began to sob and my hands shook. I could hardly breathe. Paulette handed me a box of tissues.

"In fourth grade, the kids would always tease me because I was the fattest one in the class. A group of them would pull their shirts over their noses whenever I passed by so they wouldn't breathe the same air I did. I felt humiliated, embarrassed, resentful, and angry. During this time, I found that books couldn't hurt me as much as people could."

The tears welled in my eyes, making it difficult for me to read; I quickly wiped them away, never once looking up. Clutching the paper, I made myself continue.

"I hated being at school and was constantly called names like fatso and whale. I felt hurt, embarrassed, humiliated, and angry, but I never let anyone know. I was too embarrassed to tell anyone, and I remembered my mother telling me not to let them see it bothered me. 'Don't show them how you feel.'

"I couldn't wait for lunch. I was always careful to sit with people I knew wouldn't tease me. But even they commented on how much meat my sandwiches had in them. I felt embarrassed and special. I would eat the roast-beef sandwiches slowly, savoring every bite. There would always be a piece of fruit, usually an apple, and a treat, Devil Dogs or potato chips. I thought my mother loved me more than the other kids' mothers because she packed me such great lunches and put so much meat on my sandwiches. I felt loved, deserving, and special.

"I didn't have many friends and usually felt lonely, but there was one girl, Linda, who my mother would baby-sit for after school. Whenever Linda would come over, my mother would make 'Mommy burgers,' a cheeseburger on one side with mayo on the other side with ketchup. I looked forward to Linda's visits because I knew

I would get a Mommy burger. I felt warm, loved, and excited especially since my friend could see how much my mother loved me by the good food she cooked.

"I never got to see my father very much. He usually left for work at 7:00 A.M. and came home after 7:00 P.M. We never waited to eat dinner with him. When he came home and ate his dinner, I used to wish I had another meal. I felt jealous and angry. Late at night after I was supposed to go to sleep, I could hear him in the next room eating potato chips. I would lie there and listen to him crunching. I wished I could be grown up so I could eat potato chips whenever I wanted. I felt jealous and angry.

"When I was in sixth grade, I got mono. For the first two weeks, all I could eat was ice cream, as much as I wanted and whatever kind I wanted. I felt special and loved. I was glad that I didn't have to go to school and face all the kids who would tease me. I felt comfortable and safe. After the first two weeks, I could eat anything I wanted, and because I was sick, I usually got whatever I wanted. I thought this was the perfect illness: I didn't have to go to school and I could eat anything I wanted and I didn't gain weight. I felt happy, safe, comfortable, unpressured, and loved.

"Birthdays were my favorite. I could choose whatever I wanted for dinner that night. I would begin planning my meal at least a week before and eagerly count down the days until I could have my special meal. I would pick the same thing every year, veal parmesan and french fries with a Carvel ice-cream cake. I loved the chocolate crunchies in the middle. I would eat the top and the bottom of the cake first and save the crunchy middle for last when the ice cream would be soft and creamy. I would let the ice cream slide down my throat as I crunched the chocolate insides. I felt special, happy, loved, and safe.

"All through junior high my weight increased, and I was always the fattest one in the class. I would get teased for my weight. I felt humiliated, betrayed by everyone, and worthless. I isolated myself from everyone. I read books so I could be distracted by someone else's life. I read every Nancy Drew mystery that came out. I wished everyone would love me as much as the other characters in the books loved her. I felt safe and protected.

"When I was in ninth grade, I lost almost a hundred pounds in eight months, to be at an all-time low weight of 178 pounds. I started out on a low carbohydrate, high-protein diet; then when I didn't lose enough, I would eat only a hamburger patty and an apple all day. I felt deprived, neglected, and powerful. I took Dexetrim diet pills to ease the hunger pangs. The other kids started noticing me because of my weight loss and I enjoyed the attention I was getting, especially from my dad.

"I always felt that he loved my sister more than he'd ever loved me. But now he bought me a whole new wardrobe. He would hold my hand in public when he only used to hold my sister's. I felt special and loved. I finally had my dad's full attention. It didn't seem like he loved my sister more than me.

"I hated all the comments people would make about how great I looked now. I felt angry, unworthy, and resentful. I put the weight back on almost as fast as I had lost it. I developed a craving for lollipops and decided it was cool to always have one in my mouth. The weight came back and again my dad didn't pay much attention to me. I felt abandoned, angry, and worthless.

"I tried to lose weight again several more times. I went on Weight Watchers, Slimfast, and Nutri/System. Each time I ended up putting on even more weight. I felt inadequate, worthless, and angry.

"When I was sixteen, I weighed around 250 pounds. My dad got me a job at one of the stores in the chain of grocery stores where he works. They didn't have a uniform big enough to fit me, so my mom sewed two uniforms together. I felt humiliated and embarrassed. I hated the job but I loved earning money. I got a driver's license and a car. I was ecstatic. This meant I could drive to get whatever I wanted to eat. On weeknights while I worked, I would binge on candy bars—Twix or M&M's or Reese's Peanut Butter Cups. I felt guilty, sneaky, and deserving.

"On weekend nights, I would lie to my parents and tell them I was going out with friends after work, when I was really going to McDonald's. I felt ashamed and guilty. I would order two quarter-pounders, two large fries, and two medium Diet Cokes. I ordered the two sodas so the waitress wouldn't think it was all for me. I felt sneaky, guilty, ashamed, and excited.

"I would sit in my car, in the dark, watching the other cars go by, wishing I had someone to go out and do things with. I would see the couples parked in cars and feel jealous. I always took the pickle off the quarter-pounder first and ate that with the fries. I would try to eat slow but I couldn't. I was too excited. Then I would drink the soda in between bites. After I was done, I would eat the other meal the same way. It was like a repeat of the first meal. I felt comfortable, happy, and guilty while I ate and sad, lonely, depressed, pathetic, and guilty when I was done.

"Some nights after work I would bring home a bag of potato chips or Doritos. Once when I was younger, my mom grabbed the chips from me and argued that I was on a diet and shouldn't eat them. When she took the bag away, I yelled and screamed at her to leave me alone, that

I could eat anything I wanted. I was so filled with anger.
I scared her and she gave them back to me. I was relieved. I felt guilty and excited as I ate the chips and
guilty, angry, and depressed when I had finished.

"Whenever I would bring home potato chips or Doritos or ice cream, I would sneak them into my room. I
would eat a normal-size dinner in front of my parents.
I felt angry and resentful as I ate, but excited thinking
about my treats.

"After dinner, I would sneak off to my room to watch
TV and eat. I felt excited and deserving as I went to my
room. I would eat the Doritos and the potato chips at the
same time. First, I'd eat a handful of potato chips, then a
handful of Doritos. While I was eating these, I would an-
ticipate eating the ice cream as it sat out getting softer
and creamier. I felt excited, happy, guilty, and loved as I
ate. I stuffed them in my mouth fast while drinking Tab
in between bites. When I was done with this, I'd eat the
ice cream—usually chocolate chip or Oreos and cream.

"First, I'd eat around the edges where it would be
the softest. I felt sneaky, happy, and comfortable as the
creamy, soft ice cream slid down my throat while the
chocolate crunched in my mouth. I'd continue to eat all
around the edges until I got to the center. I almost always
ate all of the half-gallon container of ice cream. I felt
guilty, lonely, depressed, and angry when I was finished.
I hated the disgusting full feeling I had and felt nauseous.

"I convinced myself that I didn't need to be out with
other people. People would only hurt me, so it was safer
staying at home in my room bingeing on weekend nights.
I still had a few friends, but I didn't have the desire to go
out with them. When I did force myself, it always seemed
to take too much energy because I would always smile
and pretend everything was great. I was always sweet and

happy, never letting anyone know how alone, isolated, and hopeless I felt.

"When I was sixteen years old, I met John. He was different from anyone I'd ever met. He was wild and he became my life. If John liked it, it was okay for me and if he didn't, I didn't like it. I met him on the phone first through a friend. I felt safe and uninhibited when we talked on the phone. He didn't know what I looked like, so I felt I could say anything. I felt scared, sad, and dishonest. I knew we would have to meet someday, and I was sure that when we did, he would hate the way I looked and hate me for never telling him how fat I was.

"The first time we tried to meet, he turned around before I could see him. I only saw the back of him as he walked away from me on the deserted street. I felt sure he had seen me and hated me. I wrote him tons of letters and called him several times a week. He wouldn't talk to me and he never answered my letters. I felt desperate, lonely, rejected, and hopeless. For the next five months, all I thought about was John—what he was doing and where he was. I talked to his friends and they told me he didn't have a girlfriend. I felt hopeful.

"I called him on Christmas Eve and he talked to me. I was ecstatic! I knew everything would be okay now. We saw each other and began doing things together. I couldn't believe how lucky I felt. I would never eat in front of him. I thought if he saw me eating, he wouldn't love me anymore. I felt ashamed, embarrassed, and sneaky. I would drive through a fast-food restaurant before or after I saw him, but never with him.

"I would eat a hot dog with bacon, a double cheeseburger, a large fry, and a large Diet Coke. I felt excited and powerful as I waited for the food. I ate in my car. I ate really fast and was careful to clean the crumbs out of the car so no one would know. I felt satisfied, sneaky, guilty, and depressed.

"My relationship with John confused me. He never kissed me except once when he was drunk. He never held my hand or said he loved me, and yet we spent all of our time together. I felt confused and rejected. I used to drive and pay whenever we went out. I felt angry and used, but I didn't break up with him. I felt trapped, desperate, and awkward.

"When John finally ended our relationship, I was devastated. I felt rejected, angry, and hopeless. I needed to prove to myself that another guy would want to touch me. I wanted to prove that I wasn't really that bad by having sex. I felt desperate, ashamed, and betrayed. I met another guy and on our second date, we had sex. I told myself I was in love with him.

"The first time we made love, I felt disappointed, unfulfilled, and inadequate. But as least I had someone to take care of me financially in the future. We started to fight about my weight and his drinking. Neither one of us could stop these behaviors. I felt sneaky, guilty, and angry as I would stop at a Duchess drive-through before I went to his house. We broke up and I felt abandoned, worthless, and angry.

"Then, I met Mike. We had sex the second time we met. I felt cheap, unfulfilled, and inadequate. I tried to convince myself that I was in love with him. He accepted my eating and ate with me. We would drive through Burger King or McDonald's and order four hamburgers, two large fries, and two large Diet Cokes and sit in the car and eat. I felt happy, comfortable, loved, and understood.

"Yet it became harder to keep up the pretext of loving Mike. I began to hate the way he reminded me of my overeating. I broke up with him and a week later, I found out I was pregnant. I was scared, confused, anxious, angry, and overwhelmed. I didn't know what to do. I only knew that if my father found out, I was sure I would get thrown out of my house. I was only seventeen years old. I didn't feel ready for a child. I had an abortion. The clinic was a nightmare. I had to go through picketers with signs saying 'Baby Killer' on them.

"The clinic was like a morgue, quiet and solemn. They put this hose up to me and it felt like they were sucking out my stomach. I hated myself. I had killed my baby and I wasn't even sure I believed in abortion."

I stopped for several seconds, quickly wiping the tears from my cheeks. I took several deep breaths. I knew the next part would be the most difficult.

"For the next three years, I isolated myself from everyone. I felt depressed, hurt, worthless, and demoralized. I would go only to work and school. The rest of the time I spent alone in my room eating. I would eat fruit-filled cookies, potato chips, Doritos, ice cream, Oreos, chocolate-chip cookies, popcorn, and chocolate bars. I felt hopeless, depressed, unworthy, demoralized, and angry. I know I ate these foods ravenously, but I don't remember actually eating them.

"During this time, my prom came up. No one asked me to go. I felt ashamed, embarrassed, worthless, and angry. I was too fat to find a gown. Whenever someone asked me if I was going to the prom, I would lie and say that my boyfriend had broken up with me so I didn't want to go. I felt guilty, self-conscious, angry, rejected, and demoralized.

"On prom night, I got potato chips, Doritos, and ice cream and repeated my ritual of eating the chips and Doritos first, then eating the ice cream after it was soft. I felt guilty, angry, and depressed.

"I started college in January. I didn't want to go to college. All I wanted to do was find a man to take care of me. The only reason I went was because my father promised to pay for half of a new car if I tried it. I stayed for four years because I had nothing better to do.

"I continued to binge on Doritos and potato chips with ice cream on weekends while I still worked at the grocery store. When I was a sophomore in college, my mother had double brain surgery—two operations in six months and a long recovery. I was the oldest child at home since my older brother lived with my grandmother, so I felt responsible for keeping things running smoothly at home. I felt scared, alone, pressured, and panicky.

"Every day I would go to the hospital and stay with a mother I no longer knew. She was quiet, withdrawn, and never talked about anything. She was a stranger to me. I felt hurt, lonely, abandoned, and angry.

"Every day when I visited the hospital, I would stop at the snack shop and get a cheeseburger, a large fry, and a vanilla milkshake. I would eat them in my mom's room. She was usually sleeping and never seemed to notice. I felt excited each day as I walked into the snack shop, and I anticipated the food on the elevator ride up. I felt excited and happy. I'd eat the cheeseburger and fries fast, sipping the shake in between. I felt guilty, happy, depressed, and anxious as I ate and angry and depressed when I was done.

"I dropped two classes to devote more time to healing my mother. And the classes I did have left seemed overwhelming. Whenever I had a paper due or a test, I would wait until the last minute to write or study. I would eat before I started researching, while I was studying or writing, and after I had finished my homework. I felt pressured, anxious, nervous, guilty, and overwhelmed. I would eat cookies, potato chips, popcorn, Devil Dogs, ice cream, and chocolate. I felt depressed, guilty, anxious, and angry after I had eaten.

"During college, I joined a sorority. I felt excited and challenged while I pledged, but I dropped out as soon as I got in. I didn't feel I belonged when they were being nice to me. I couldn't understand why they wanted me as a member. I felt inadequate, lonely, and depressed.

"I quit working at the grocery store and began working as an editorial assistant at a weekly paper. I was excited. On weekends, I was the only one at work. All I could think about was food. I would never leave the office to get food. Instead, I would eat whatever was around and when I couldn't find anything sitting out, I would rummage through other people's desks. I felt driven, guilty, and justified.

"Once, I found several small candy bars in this lady's desk. I felt excited. I was sure she wouldn't miss them. There weren't many. I felt angry that she had only seven candy bars in her desk. I left four. I ate two slowly, trying to make the taste last. I felt guilty, happy, angry, and sneaky. I tried to sit down and concentrate on work, but all I could think about was the candy. I felt driven and angry.

"I went back and got two more candy bars and ate them fast. I felt unsatisfied, angry, guilty, and depressed. I knew I couldn't eat them all, so I left work right after. I felt unsatisfied, angry, guilty, and ashamed.

"After I graduated, I went away to graduate school in Syracuse, New York. I knew I wanted to write. I felt excited that I had finally figured out what I wanted to do after four years of just getting by. I felt hopeful and scared.

"When I moved to Syracuse, my parents took me grocery shopping. I bought what I thought was diet food. They spent $100 on groceries for me. I got hot dogs, hamburgers, cheese, fruit, salad, cereal, and popcorn. I felt excited and free. I was away from home. I could eat whatever I wanted. I had only one roommate and she went away on weekends. I would plan what I would eat when she wasn't there.

"I would make two Mommy burgers and popcorn and grab a bag of potato chips. I felt loved, safe, warm, and guilty while I ate, and angry, lonely, and depressed when I had finished.

"I felt lonely and scared in a strange place with no one I knew. It seemed like everyone else was doing so much and having fun while I would stay in my apartment and eat. I convinced myself that I didn't need to have fun. I had too much work to do. I felt lonely, inadequate, unloved, and desperate.

"I couldn't do the work I had. I couldn't remember enough information to get any better than a C on a test, and my papers were not sufficiently researched. My grades were just barely passing. I felt angry, guilty, stupid, and inadequate.

"I would go home on some weekends. I knew my mother would cook special meals for me. She would make roast beef, pot roast, or meatballs with mashed potatoes. I felt warm and loved. I knew I would get the leftovers to take back with me. I felt excited. I would eat two roast-beef sandwiches on the way back to school and McDonald's food on the way home. I always had the same thing. I felt deserving, happy, guilty, and depressed.

"Once on the ride back to Syracuse, I was intent on getting my roast-beef sandwich out. I wasn't paying attention to the road or my speed; when I did look in the rearview mirror, a police car had its lights on. I got a ticket for going seventy-five miles per hour. I had no idea how fast I was going.

"In the fall, I decided it was time I learned how to cook. I bought two cookbooks and read them all the time. I enjoyed looking at the pictures and felt excited to see how good the food looked. I invited people over for dinner. I would cook huge amounts so there'd be leftovers that I could eat after everyone left. I made fried chicken, mashed potatoes, stew, french fries, steak, hamburgers, and hot dogs. We had chocolate mousse pie or ice cream and Kahlúa for dessert.

"I felt angry and ashamed that I had to eat slowly and have small portions in front of these people. I felt resentful and could not concentrate on the conversations. All I could think about was what I would eat when they left. I would get angry if someone ate too much, but I held it all in. I felt angry, resentful, insincere, and dishonest.

"If they stayed after dinner, for a movie or to talk, I would sometimes pretend to be tired so they would leave and I could be alone to eat. I would eat the whole meal over again, this time eating as much as I wanted. I felt satisfied, lonely, and inadequate.

"Once when my thin friend Wendy came over to watch movies, I made a huge bowl of popcorn dripping with butter. She said I had made too much for just the two of us. I didn't care what she thought. She ate only a little and I ate the rest. I felt embarrassed, guilty, depressed, and powerless. I felt angry and resentful when she didn't want to eat with me anymore.

"I arranged my class schedule so I could be home during the afternoons. I would binge during my soap operas. I would be excited during the morning, looking forward to watching my soaps and eating. I would eat from 12:30

to 4:00 P.M., taking several breaks in between. I would eat Mommy burgers, popcorn, potato chips, M&M's, pizza, peanut butter with crackers, and ice cream. I felt comfortable, lonely, safe, depressed, angry, and guilty while eating and depressed, hopeless, angry, and powerless after. In the late afternoon, I would usually have to take a nap to get rid of the bloated, full feeling I had. I felt gluttonous.

"I started counseling at the urging of my sister. I was desperate and scared. After I had been to a few self-help meetings, suggested by my counselor, I would binge on salad loaded with parmesan cheese, fruit, and fruit salad. I felt justified and deserving. I told myself that this was healthy food and since I was a compulsive overeater, I just couldn't stop myself. I felt hopeless and deserving.

"During this time, I fell in love with Tim. He was everything I was looking for—strong, secure, emotionally closed, and a challenge. I put all my energy into pleasing him. He was in my every thought. I would cook huge meals for him, but I would eat small portions while he was there. Before Tim would come over, I would always hide anything that could possibly reveal how much I ate.

"Once I made chocolate-chip cookies for Tim. He loved them. They were big and soft on the inside and crunchy around the edges. He talked about the cookies for days. After that, I would use any excuse I could find to make him cookies—holidays, birthdays, a bad day, or just because I wanted to. One time, I made eighteen dozen and passed them out to friends. I made sure I kept three or four dozen for myself. I would eat two cookies after breakfast, two after lunch, two before dinner, and four after dinner. I loved the way the chocolate melted in my mouth.

"After I had made cookies for Tim about six or eight

times, he told me that he'd had enough. I didn't understand. I was devastated, hurt, and sad. I was afraid he
wouldn't spend any more time with me. I didn't want
to be alone. I felt scared, lonely, and desperate.

"We still spent time together, but not as often now.
I only saw him every couple of weeks. I never told him
how I felt about him. I would binge before and after seeing him.

"After every encounter with Tim, I ate. I couldn't stop
and I hated myself for it. I would order a large bacon
pizza from Dominos for lunch and eat the whole thing
by dinner. A few hours later, I would cook hamburgers,
hot dogs, kielbasa, and steak out on the grill. I would eat
two hot dogs, two hamburgers, a piece of kielbasa, and a
piece of steak. I felt lonely, depressed, scared, hopeless,
and powerless. I hated eating so much, and I knew I was
spending too much of my parents' money—about $100
a week—on groceries.

"I got bronchitis for three weeks. I couldn't eat for the
first two weeks. I was shocked. Never before had I been
not able to eat. I tried to eat clam chowder at the beginning of the third week. My stomach couldn't take it and
I threw it up. It didn't matter. I wanted to eat. I ate and
hoped my stomach would settle. I thought it was great
that I could eat anything I wanted and not gain weight.
I hated the way my face got red and my eyes watered
when I threw up, but I needed to eat more. I felt angry,
scared, and hopeful that I could eat more.

"Right after I got better, Tim told me that he didn't
have a need to talk to me and that his life was fine with
me and fine without me. I felt worthless, devastated, and
dejected. I tried to stay away from him, but that lasted
for only a month. I had to see him. I went to his apart-

ment. He acted like nothing had happened. I felt confused, frustrated, and angry.

"I tried not to see him anymore, and I went a few
weeks without seeing him. During this time I called Glenbeigh after a friend recommended the hospital. A few
days before I came here, I wrote Tim a letter, telling him
that I had fallen in love with him and that he had hurt
me very much. I baked him chocolate-chip cookies and
gave them to him with the letter. I felt excited and happy
when I saw him and sad, depressed, and hurt when I had
gone. I knew that after he read the letter, things would be
different between us.

"After I knew I was going to Glenbeigh, I spent a lot of
money. I would go to the mall and buy things, anything:
stuff for my apartment, towels, pot holders, shelves, a
table. I would order clothes from Lane Bryant and Roa-
man's, sometimes spending seventy dollars or so at time.
I would split the bill on two credit cards so my father
wouldn't get angry. I felt excited, guilty, and happy.

"When my mother visited me, we went shopping.
I used her credit card to buy all the things I needed to
come to Glenbeigh and a lot of stuff I didn't really need.
I felt excited, guilty, and depressed.

"A few days before I left, my friend Mark came over
and we ordered a medium pizza. I felt angry and resentful that he only wanted a medium pizza. I ate slowly,
ladylike, in front of him. I felt fake and deceitful.

"When we were finished, he said he was still hungry
and suggested we get another pizza. I was excited. I felt
safe, warm, understood, resentful, ashamed, embarrassed
that I had eaten so much, and angry.

"We got the other pizza and I again ate slowly. I felt
angry, resentful, and fake. Two pieces were left and he

wanted to throw them out, but I yelled no and quickly put them in the refrigerator. I felt happy and excited.

"He stayed for a while longer, but all I could think about was the pizza. I wanted him to leave. I felt angry and hateful. The minute he left, I attacked the pizza. I felt angry and unsatisfied when I was done; I wanted more and there wasn't any.

"The day before I came here, I was angry and resentful that my friends, some whom I wouldn't see ever again, wouldn't leave me alone. I didn't want them at my apartment. I felt angry, resentful, and hateful. There was at least one person there all the time. I didn't care about saying good-bye. All I wanted to do was eat. I saved a chocolate brownie for after they left. It was late and I hated the brownie. I hated all food because of the pain it had caused me. I threw it away.

"I left my apartment to come to Glenbeigh at 7:00 A.M. the next morning. I was too nervous to eat the morning before leaving. I was afraid I'd get sick on the plane. I ate a dry piece of French toast on the plane. I didn't even like the way it tasted. I felt angry that my last food was so unsatisfying. I felt angry, depressed, and unsatisfied.

"On the plane, my seat belt wouldn't fit around me. I was too embarrassed to ask for a seat-belt extender, so I held my hands over the clasp so the stewardess wouldn't know. I felt humiliated, embarrassed, guilty, and depressed."

Staring at the paper for a second, I slowly looked up at Linda. I didn't want to, but I'd heard enough of these to know that if I continued to look down, she would tell me to make eye contact. As I met her eyes, she waved her index finger in a circular motion, indicating that I should look at the others. Taking a deep breath as the tears once again began to well up in my eyes, I slowly met each person's eyes. Instead of the hatred I had expected, I saw smiles of encouragement, nods of understanding, and genuine emotion as I made my way around the circle.

Halfway around, I saw Georgia. She had arrived here only a few days ago. She was a little heavier than me, but about the same age. She sat huddled in a mass on the sofa sobbing, her dark, shoulder-length hair all but covering her face.

For the first time, I understood her pain. It was similar to mine. At more than three hundred pounds, we had both suffered at the hands of vicious remarks from people disgusted by the size of our bodies. We had been humiliated and morally bankrupted by our addiction, losing both our self-respect and dignity to a hidden disease neither of us could name until this very moment in this room.

Once again, my eyes began to fill up with tears. I cried for all of the pain I'd suffered as a victim of food addiction. I cried for all the times I had wanted so desperately for someone to accept me just as I was—fat. But, most of all, I cried for the complete powerlessness I'd felt. Despite all of my attempts, dieting and otherwise, there was no way I could have changed things until I knew what I was up against.

Without understanding my addiction to sugar, flour, and fats, I was helpless to stop overeating. If I could have changed my situation, I would have. All those years, all that pain. Being fat, hating every inch of my body. Feeling absolutely humiliated, beaten by food. These are things that, given the choice, I would not have wanted for my life.

I finally understood what the people here meant about acknowledging our powerlessness over food, yet still taking responsibility for our actions. Before I came here, I didn't understand or know about my addiction, but now that I do, it's up to me to do the work to stay in recovery. Right now, today, it's my choice about the future. I am no longer food's unknowing victim.

"Thank you for sharing your First Step, Debbie," Linda cleared her throat and continued. "Who would like to give Debbie some feedback?"

I cringed. As the tears streamed down my face, I clutched my notebook. In my hands I held my most humiliating secrets that were now in the open.

Looking at the people in this room, I wanted to run away from these clones of myself. They had this disease too, and I hated them for being constant reminders of my weakness, my pain.

"Thank you, Debbie, for sharing your First Step with me." My thoughts were interrupted by Krista, a very thin, young girl who suffered from bulimia. "I could relate to a lot of what you said, especially with all of the relationships and the self-hatred. I felt sad listening to your pain, but I was really amazed by the amounts of food you ate in one sitting. It was just incredible. Thanks again for sharing."

When she had finished, I matched her smile, though I wasn't sure about what she had said. Had she just called me a pig?

Before Linda called on someone else, she turned her attention to Georgia. Since I had finished reading, Georgia's sobs had grown stronger and louder, into a deep animal sound.

"What's going on, Georgia?" Linda's voice was determined and firm without any trace of sympathy.

"I . . . I'm . . . I don't know. I . . ." Georgia's voice drifted off into loud sobs. After a few seconds, she began to speak again between her sobs. "I'm just so confused. I . . . All those people who teased me. I just couldn't stop eating. I wanted to be thin so much." Georgia wasn't able to speak anymore. Her layers of fat shook as she cried.

"That's good, Georgia. Get it all out. Ellen, did you have your hand up?"

Turning to face my new roommate, I saw that her eyes were red and her cheeks damp.

Before speaking, Ellen cleared her throat. "Debbie, I just want to thank you for sharing your First Step. I admire your courage and your honesty, and I could really relate to the huge amounts of food you ate. I did the same thing. . . ." Ellen's voice trailed off as she wiped a tear from her cheek. "I'm just so grateful that you're my roommate. I think we'll learn a lot from each other."

The next half hour became a blur of people thanking me and commenting about the things they could relate to in my First Step. Even though I had heard these people talk about these subjects before, there was something different about today. This time, they were sharing what they had related to in my story.

I had no idea how freeing it could be to hear their comments. Smiling, I slowly looked around the circle to meet each person's eyes. They had all given me something I had never in my life known—unconditional love and acceptance.

The minute they had finished, I heard Linda's voice. Now, it was time for her to tell me what she thought. One word from her and I would have to do this whole thing again. If your First Step wasn't accepted, you had to redo it. I held my breath as she began to speak.

"I love you, Debbie, and thank you. You were very in touch with your feelings. I didn't hear any self-pity or shame, and your honesty is admirable. I believe that you are very clear about the devastation your disease has caused, and that will serve you well in your recovery. You've still got a lot of work to do, but you've also come a long way with acknowledging your feelings. Okay, everyone, that's it for now. Let's close."

As members of the group slowly rose and held hands, I looked up to the ceiling and said a silent prayer of thanks. For the first time since I came here, I truly understood what it meant to turn my will and my life over to a Power greater than myself. From the minute I started reading, I had completely let go of my own will, trusting what I believed to be God's. And though it was scary, it certainly turned out better than I had ever imagined.

◆ *Day 22* ◆

July 24, 1989

Everyone was really nice to me today. Thankfully, they were polite, but kept their distance. I have no desire to talk to anyone. I just feel so exhausted. It was all I could do to get up and start the day. Oh, how I wished I could wake up in my own bed at a reasonable hour, instead of here in this stark white room with a virtual stranger.

Last night, I made my first phone call to my parents. It was so good to hear their voices. They kept asking me if I was okay and telling me how good I was doing. I really needed to hear that. About half an hour later, I called my sister. Even though I wanted to talk to Mark, I needed to hear my sister's voice. I didn't realize how much I missed talking to her until last night. At least now I feel stronger and even more anxious to get out of here.

There was another First Step today. It was Michelle's. She came here the same day I did. I felt so sad for her while she read. Food had done a lot of destruction in her life too. Like Tracy, Michelle had seriously thought about and even tried to leave in the beginning, but look

139

at her now. Her counselor accepted her First Step, just like mine did.

I didn't say much to Michelle after she was done reading. It was hard for me to even concentrate on what she was saying. I just feel so out of it, so raw and spent. It's as if my insides have been ripped out. Everything I kept inside for all those years is out of me, and there's really nothing to replace it. Without these secrets, I don't even know who I am. It's a scary, empty feeling to realize how little there is in my life without food and overeating. I can't think about this anymore now or I'll go crazy.

I want to do the questions and go to sleep. One question is to list all the attempts I've made to control my food addiction and describe how I felt at the time and now.

	now	then
Weight Watchers	angry	hopeful, frustrated
High-carbo/low-protein diet	angry	hopeful, frustrated
Slimfast	angry	hopeful, frustrated
Nutri/System	angry	hopeful, frustrated
Self-restricting	angry	hopeful, frustrated

◆ Day 23 ◆

July 25, 1989

I really wanted to keep to myself again today, but Donna, the recreational therapist, wouldn't let me. Everything was going okay until 4:30 this afternoon at recreation. I really hate the stupid games we have to play—basketball, baseball, and so on—but they are nothing compared with what we had to do today when we met in the family room.

Donna called it a "trust walk." She had us count off into six groups. Then Donna chose a leader for each group. When she approached our group, I looked down at the floor.

"Debbie," she said loudly, "you're the leader for your group."

My heart raced.

"Okay. Leaders, what you're going to do is just that— lead," she said and then laughed.

I hated her for that.

"It's up to you to lead the other five people in your group safely through the obstacles we have set up through-out the unit and outside. Everyone except for the leaders

141

will be blindfolded and you'll all hold on to each other's waists."

Looking over my group, I was horrified to find that Jean was among the members. In her late fifties, Jean was extremely overweight and walked with a cane. How was I supposed to lead her through anything without killing her?

Angrily, I helped my group line up the way we were instructed to. I was careful not to get too close to Jean. She hadn't been here that long and I didn't know her very well. I wanted to keep it that way. I hated sick people. My grandmother was a sick person, and I couldn't stand to listen to her moan about her aches and pains.

Like Jean, my grandmother needed help to walk, or so she said; she used a walker. Also like Jean, my grandmother was overweight and had white-and-black hair and glasses. Jean's pudgy cheeks, wrinkled skin, and bad hearing also reminded me of my grandmother.

When my grandmother moved in with us four years ago, I had hated every minute of it. The mood of our once-quiet house became dominated by my grandmother's sicknesses, imagined or real. Now here I was taking care of her once more, only in a different form.

As I walked down the line of people, I checked each one to make sure their blindfolds were in place. Then I studied the area that was laid out in front of me. The first obstacle to lead my group through was a narrow door with a step down to the outside.

My heart pounded as the group in front of us began its journey. In a matter of two minutes, it would be time to lead my group. My palms were sweaty as I positioned Krista's hands around my waist. Slowly, I took my first step as everyone behind me followed. Reaching for the door, I instructed Krista to step down and continue forward, turning slightly to the right.

As each person followed, I gave instructions to step down until it was Jean's turn. At the end of the line, she slowly hobbled up to the door. With sweat pouring off my brow, I loudly instructed Jean to step down. Putting one of her arms onto the door handle, I grabbed her other arm, directing the cane down the step. She moved slowly as I nervously glanced at the others who were stopped. What did they think? What were they feeling standing blindly outside without any guidance?

Forcing myself to be patient, even though I wanted to scream wildly at this woman to hurry up, I slowly led Jean down the step to join the others. Then, linked together by our arms, we continued slowly around the building to the far entrance. Continually looking over my shoulder, I tried to ensure that our path was free of branches and rocks.

Though the sun beat down strongly, I had no time to enjoy it; I needed to help my group turn right. Taking baby steps so Jean could keep up, I stopped the group just before another set of steps. I could feel Krista's nails digging deeply into my waist as I told her to step up. I was grateful to see that the door was open wide.

"Walk through a doorway, take a few steps, and stop," I told Krista as she walked carefully.

Holding each person's arm on the steps up, I was careful to slow the group down enough to allow Jean time to approach the steps.

"Okay, Jean, there's a step here," I said loudly and grabbed her arm. "You're right in front of it; just lift your leg and hold on here." I directed her arm to the door handle as she hoisted her large body up the step.

Returning to the head of the line, I was horrified to see a maze of chairs and mesh obstacles before us. How was I going to get these people through such a mess? Taking a deep breath, I slowly led the group around the first chair, then glared at Donna as I saw her holding the mesh up to waist level. She had to be insane to think that Jean could squat to pass underneath.

"Donna. Jean . . . What should I do?"

"I'll take her," she said to me. "Jean, come over here and wait for your group."

Slowly, one by one, beginning with Krista, I instructed my group members to kneel and crawl under the mesh. Walking around to the other side, I grabbed Krista's hand when she had finished and helped her up. I did this with each person until we were once again in our line with Jean at the end.

Next, I led the group past the nurses' station, once again being careful to walk at a maddeningly slow pace for Jean's sake. Taking a right turn, we were directed to return to the family room, where I was told to seat my group.

"Okay, everyone take off your blindfolds," Donna said several minutes after we were seated. "How is everyone doing?"

After a garbled response, she asked, "Who would like to share their feelings?"

After one woman talked about being afraid to walk while blindfolded, Krista raised her hand.

"I felt angry while we were doing this," she said. "Debbie kept talking us through it, but I wanted to hear more from her. And I was so impatient with how slow we were moving. I could see how hard it was for me to give up control and trust that Debbie would lead us safely back."

After one other person spoke about being afraid, I raised my hand.

"I felt overwhelmed with responsibility," I said, careful to talk only about my own feelings, even though I wanted to tell Krista how stupid she was. "I found that it was very hard to be responsible for these people's safety. I just wanted to be a member of the group, not the leader. And I also realized that I didn't trust myself enough to take care of them."

"That's a good observation," Donna said, smiling at me.

While I was shocked at what had come out of my mouth, I really didn't care what she thought. I just wanted to be left alone. On top of everything I had been through the past few days, I learned that I didn't even trust myself. Just one more thing to "work on," as they put it in here, now that I'm getting so "healthy." It sure doesn't feel like it. Actually, I almost feel worse than when I came here but there's nothing I can do about that now except end this day by doing the questions.

I have to list what I do well in my life: I am a good writer. I get along well with people. I can be a good student and I am a hard worker.

Now, I have to discuss how I feel that my intelligence is worthless when it comes to my food addiction. I feel angry, frustrated, confused, humble, and scared by the fact that my intelligence is worth nothing to overcome my merciless obsession.

Finally, I have to write about the issues I wish to work on. I wish to work on writing the anger letter to my grandmother that I was assigned during group. It is important for me to leave my stored-up anger here and not take it home with me.

◆ Day 24 ◆

July 26, 1989

I think I'm growing a little bit in here. Today during group something strange happened that I never would have been able to handle before. A few days ago, Craig, a rotund, burly guy with beautiful blue eyes, joined the group. He had been pretty quiet up until today and I hardly noticed him when I was preoccupied with doing my First Step.

Today, he had to read one of his assignments, an anger letter to the disease. And the more he read, the angrier he got. His chubby face turned red and his eyes bulged as he clenched the paper in front of him. By the time he had gotten halfway through, he was yelling.

A few seconds later, Phil stopped him from reading and handed him a pillow. Kneeling on the floor in the middle of the circle, Craig gently hit the pillow against the floor.

"Harder! Harder! Think about how much you hate this disease!" Phil shouted and Craig began to pound the pillow against the floor.

"I hate this disease! I hate it for robbing me of my life!

I hate this disease!" Craig yelled, now viciously beating the pillow. Bam! Bam! Bam!

I was, at first, terrified of his anger. Such a big man could be dangerous if he lost control, and what did I really know about Craig? As I looked around the room, it appeared that I was not alone in my feelings. Several other women were crying and one even turned away from Craig.

But, as he continued pounding the pillow, I was amazed at how calm I became. After a few seconds of terror, I began to see Craig not as a dangerous man, but as a suffering food addict. His anger was the result of his disease, not of his masculinity. Craig had the same anger I did. The only difference was that he was a man.

As Craig finished and raised his head to look around at the group, I was able to meet his eyes and smile at him. He had made a big step toward releasing some of his pent-up anger and that wasn't an easy thing to do. His anger was no threat to me. It was directed at only one person: himself. I know that truly is a miracle for me to see.

This is the first bit of hope I've had since doing my First Step. I'm hoping that some of my sadness is passing, so that time will move faster. I can't wait to leave here. I would kill to have an hour all to myself without having to be somewhere or with someone. One of the hardest parts about being here is that I have no privacy. I never realized how lucky I was in the outside world.

Time for the questions. First, I have to reread the section in the AA book on page 53 that begins, "Arrived at this point, we were squarely confronted with the question of faith," then write about faith and trust in my life. I have faith in and trust my Higher Power. I trust that He won't give me more than I can handle. I have faith that He will always be there and that He has a plan for my life. I also trust the process of the program here as well as the people here and have faith in them.

Now I have to discuss how spiritual principles can solve my problems if I learn to trust. I trust that God will always take care of me and never give me more than I can handle. Because I believe that God already has a plan for me, it seems senseless to worry about things obsessively anymore.

Next, I have to write a prayer that is personal to me and that I can use to contact God. Here goes:

> God, I turn my will and my life over to you. Please give me the strength, knowledge, and courage to do Your will. Help me to be abstinent today and please help me to be tolerant, patient, kind, and free from anger.

Finally, I need to discuss my discomfort about prayer and meditation. I still feel a little embarrassed kneeling in front of my roommate, but we prayed together last night with other people and it felt good. I need to understand meditation a little more, but I am not uncomfortable with the idea of it.

I also heard two sayings today that I want to remember:

> Dear Debbie,
> I don't need your help today.
>
> > Love,
> > God

and

> "I have to stay on the program every day because that's the price I pay for freedom."

Nineteen days left until I can experience *real* freedom from this place. I'm starting my countdown tomorrow.

◆ *Day 25* ◆

July 27, 1989
(18 days left)

I heard a short prayer the other day that I've been saying to myself when I wake up: "God, please help me to remember that nothing is going to happen today that you and I can't get through together." In a strange way, it comforts me. My moods in here are so unpredictable. Like today. One minute I was laughing, so relieved that my First Step was over, and the next I was crying and screaming.

We did something unusual this morning. Instead of going to our individual family groups, we all gathered for big family group. The counselors had decided that we all needed to express our anger together. They said they've seen a lot of anger around here and it was time we dealt with it.

Gathered in a huge circle, we read our assignments on anger. They started preparing us for this group by giving us anger work a few days ago. Knowing that made me even more nervous about what they plan behind our backs. Phil began by asking for volunteers to read their assignments. No one spoke up until, Billy, one of the guys—now we were up to five with another one coming tomorrow—volunteered to read his anger letter to the disease.

"I hate you for robbing me of my life. I hate you for taking away everything good in my life. I hate you for making sex with my wife so difficult." As his voice trailed off, Phil directed him to the center of the circle and handed him a pillow. Billy's loud voice echoed throughout the room and his layers of fat shook each time he struck the pillow against the floor.

I began to feel my own anger well up inside as my thoughts turned to my grandmother. My disease had gotten really out of control after I moved to Syracuse for graduate school. I chose that school because I didn't want to live with her anymore. If she weren't there, I would have gone on living with my parents.

What I really hated, though, was that my father had allowed her to live there despite my feelings. He had chosen her over me. Clenching my fists, I quickly looked around for a pillow as an overwhelming wave of anger rushed to the surface. Phil, noticing my actions, quickly ran over to my side.

"Okay. Get it all out! Let it go!" He grabbed a pillow and pulled a chair over for me as I began to scream.

"I hate her for ruining my life! I hate her for all the pain she's caused me! I hate her for always being so sick! I hate her sickness!" Pounding the pillow, I could barely catch my breath as I continued. "And I hate my father for choosing her over me! I hate him for that! I hate him for letting her live in our house! For letting her spoil our family."

As my breathing grew heavier, I couldn't get the words out anymore. Coughing and choking, I tried desperately to speak, but I couldn't. Instead, I continued to pound the pillow violently against the chair.

"That's it. Get it all out!" Phil yelled to be heard over my coughing.

Just as I was about to speak, I opened my mouth and a gush of phlegm came out. I was mortified. I had thrown up in front of all these people! Stunned, I stopped beating the pillow.

"No, don't stop," Phil yelled. "It's okay. We'll wipe it up. Don't worry. Just keep going!"

I continued to yell and scream, a deep animal sound from the core of my being, as I beat the pillow against the chair. And, to my horror, I threw up again. This time I did as Phil had instructed. I kept beating the pillow until I could no longer move my arms.

Spent, I looked up to see several other people beating pillows and screaming. Taking a deep breath, I leaned back in my chair. I had no more energy for anything.

Luckily, no one said anything about this episode to me today. I'm hoping they didn't notice, but I'm sure they did. I've never seen anyone get sick from doing anger work. I feel so foolish. I have so little control over my emotions that it scares me. How could I become so angry and not be able to stop it? I could always control my feelings before I came here. This is just another thing this place has taken from me. Hopefully, things will seem better in the morning.

July 28, 1989

(17 days left)

Today was quiet compared with the past several days.
We saw a film about food addiction with Phil in it.
Mostly he just lectured about the physical aspects of the
disease. He described how years of eating foods filled
with sugar and flour affect a person's brain chemistry. I
didn't understand all of it, but I did get that once the addict stops eating those foods, the body returns to normal
and physical cravings stop.

One of the most interesting facts in the video was that
it takes twenty-one days to detoxify from sugar and flour.
At that point, the brain begins to manufacture a chemical
called serotonin that it had once gotten from the food. I
know I heard this when I first came in, but it made more
sense to me today.

I've been here a little longer than twenty-one days
and I feel drastically different now. Surprisingly, I'm not
constantly thinking about or craving food. I feel as if
I've lost a hundred pounds already. I know it sounds
silly, but I feel so much lighter. Not only physically, but

emotionally too. While I still want to leave in a big way, I can see the good that being here has done for me already.

One of the nicest things is that I'm not as afraid as I was when I first came here. After everything I've been through, I am starting to believe that I can handle almost anything as far as my feelings are concerned. By reading my First Step and surviving, I proved to myself that I am a strong person. I have and am facing my demons, and so far they haven't gotten the best of me.

I may not like it here, especially the rigid schedule, but it is working like nothing else ever has. None of those other diets I tried ever mentioned a physical addiction or an emotional connection to my weight problem. All those years I blamed myself for my incredible weakness, and it wasn't my fault at all. I have a brain-chemical imbalance that can be treated. That and the way I now feel are examples of the miracles they talk about here.

Today, I can honestly say that I know what it feels like to be grateful. And I don't mean the kind of false gratitude I used to feel when I got something I wanted. This gratitude doesn't come from material things. It's a deep down, gut-level feeling that I can't even begin to explain. All I can say is that it is an all-consuming feeling I've never experienced before.

July 29, 1989
(16 days left)

The most amazing thing happened today during journal group. It gives me goose bumps just thinking about it. It all began at 11:30 A.M. Since it's Saturday, we didn't have family group. Instead, Linda led us in a journal group, and Kathy shared her assignment.

Kathy's loud, gravelly voice and angry attitude scare me, so I stay away from her. And ever since she yelled during group a few weeks ago about not believing in God because there are starving children in the world, I have been really afraid of her.

Kathy's assignment was to write a help-wanted ad for a new Higher Power. Before Kathy began reading, Linda told us that we can change our concept of God anytime we want, that we don't have to accept the concept of God we have always believed. My heart began to race as anger poured out of Kathy's eyes when Linda told her to begin. I was afraid she would snap and begin swinging at people. I held my breath. To my surprise, her voice was low as she began to read. This is part of what she read:

God Wanted

Someone to hold my hand when things get rough.
Someone to poke me when I'm too tough.

Someone to hold me when I feel insecure.
Someone to talk to when I'm not sure.

Someone to love that I can call mine.

When Kathy was done reading, no one spoke for several seconds. It was the first time I had ever seen Linda, or any of the counselors for that matter, speechless. Everyone asked Kathy for a copy of her poem. I think it was the first time I ever saw Kathy smile.

While I am really grateful to see her growth, part of me is jealous, really jealous. I mean, here's this woman who never wrote a thing in her life and she comes along today with a masterpiece. What does that say about me and all of the years I've tried to get my writing published?

When I was an undergraduate, I had an article published in *Seventeen* magazine. That was the biggest thing I'd ever done. But I've certainly never written anything as beautiful as Kathy did today. After the *Seventeen* article, I sent out a few more manuscripts, but none were accepted, so I gave up. I know now that I chose to eat instead.

The only writing I've done lately has been term papers for school. And I want to be a writer more than anything. I just can't seem to write anymore. It's so painful to face my failure, and hearing Kathy's poem reminded me of just how long it's been since I wrote anything worthwhile.

I'm jealous of her, too, because of the feelings behind the poem. I don't feel that way about God. I never even considered that anyone could. To me, God has always been this punishing force outside of myself, a thing I would pray to so I would lose weight or when I was in serious trouble, like when my mother had surgery.

Kathy's description of God as a friend was something I had never even imagined. God was this all-powerful force whom I always tried hard not to bother, except when things got too rough. Then my praying was always short and to the point. Even with all of this praying I've been doing lately, I still never thought of God as a friend. It just blows me away that Kathy feels like that. I only hope that someday I will too.

July 30, 1989
(15 days left)

For the first time in twenty-eight days, I experienced true freedom! I was finally allowed to go to the mall. I had an assignment to do while I was there, but I did have some time to shop. It was a little hard smelling all the foods, especially the popcorn—that was my assignment: smell several foods and write how I felt. I barely noticed the food though, because it was so great to be in the stores again, to be like a normal person.

Before I went, I committed to Ellen—she went too—that I would buy only one shirt and nothing else. I was afraid of getting crazy with my spending again. And the most amazing thing—I'm in a smaller size! I don't have to wear a size fifty-two anymore! It felt so good to go into Lane Bryant and not look at the biggest size they have!

I bought a beautiful black-and-white striped blouse in a size forty-eight! The sleeves fold up from the wrists to the elbows and are held there by a strip of black-and-white fabric buttoned over each sleeve. It was the coolest thing! This is the shirt I'm going to wear when I leave Glenbeigh.

A wonderful thing is starting to happen with my body. I haven't wanted to say anything before because I was afraid to jinx it, but I have to admit it now that everyone else keeps mentioning it. I'm starting to lose some serious weight, though I have no idea how much. We still get on the scale backward on Mondays, but my jeans are getting to be quite baggy!

I feel completely overwhelmed when I think of being a normal-size person. Yet I can hardly wait to experience that. It's been more than nine years since I've been at a decent weight. I don't even remember what it feels like.

When I lost all that weight in junior high school, I ate only an apple and a plain hamburger all day and exercised five miles on a stationary bicycle. I felt like a princess. My parents bought me all new clothes and I looked beautiful, but when I put the weight back on, those clothes became painful reminders of my failure.

I also remember that people who had never bothered with me before started to talk to me. The popular girls began to say hello and some of the guys even noticed me. The attention was overwhelming, though I didn't realize it.

I don't want this shirt to become another painful re- minder. If this program doesn't work, I don't know what else there is. I'm afraid I will die from being so fat. Before coming here, that's how I always thought it would be— I'd die alone and fat.

Sure, it was hard to smell the food, especially the pop- corn. I used to eat popcorn every day. But none of that food smelled better than how I feel. I feel different now, more serious, than when I was dieting. If I eat food with sugar and flour in it today, I know there's a chance I may never stop eating because of my body chemistry. Before it was just a matter of gaining a pound or two and what did that matter at my weight?

I see all those foods as my enemies now, not as the comfort they used to be. Today, that food is what will cause my destruction and I know it. Before I came here, I couldn't have stopped eating because I didn't know about my addiction. And I don't ever want to lose this clear-headed feeling. No food is worth that.

During group yesterday we cut out pictures of our binge foods from magazines to make a collage. It scares me to think about what they have in store for us with this one. Somehow this seems as if I am going backward. I came here to get away from these foods, not dwell on them. Nevertheless, I will do as they say so I can leave on time.

I also heard that we got a new guy today while I was at the mall. He's supposed to be enormous. I'm sure I'll meet him soon enough. Well, I have to do the questions now and get some sleep. I can hardly wait to wear my new blouse because that means I'll be leaving!

July 31, 1989
(14 days left)

I woke up this morning really excited. Two weeks from today I leave here! That was all I could think about at breakfast and through most of the morning. And to top it all off, I didn't have any really hard assignments. Then I went to see the psychiatrist and everything changed.

For insurance purposes, we are required to meet once every other week with a psychiatrist. Usually, it's a nothing visit. I go in, he asks me how I'm doing and if I'm having any problems, I say no, then I leave. Our visits are so brief that I don't even know his name.

Today, however, he hesitated for a moment while he read my chart. I sat there wringing my hands together. Rubbing his temples, he looked me directly in the eyes.

"There's some concern among the staff about your progress. They seem to be afraid that you're not working as hard as you first were," he said. "The counselors think you have given up on your recovery."

My heart nearly stopped. How could they say that I wasn't working on my recovery? Just being in this horrible place meant that I was doing something right. My face reddened and I looked down. The doctor flipped through more pages of my chart.

"Ah, it says here that they aren't as worried anymore. You must have started working again." I could feel his eyes studying me, but I refused to meet his gaze. "Don't worry. It's okay now."

"Oh, you mean after I did my First Step," I said, forcing myself not to reveal my feelings. "After that, I just needed to rest. I was so exhausted. . . ."

And that was it. Within minutes the meeting was over. It was only my fears that lingered. Just the other day I heard that the counselors were thinking of keeping another patient an extra week or two!

Without a doubt that is my biggest fear. I really believe I would die if I had to stay here longer than six weeks. I can't keep living like this for much longer.

I hate being told when to eat and having to ask a nurse for my razor every night just to shave my legs. I can't stand getting up at six every morning, knowing that I'm going to spend the next twenty-four hours trapped here.

I'm so jealous of the people I saw at the mall yesterday. They're going about their normal lives, not realizing how lucky they are to come and go as they please. They don't have to find a buddy just to walk outside or down the hall. They don't have to be locked up just to learn how to eat normally, and they can eat whatever they want whenever they want. How I hate them for that.

I hate this damn disease! It stole years of my life and made me feel like a weak failure. It made me hate myself and everything else in my life. And it took away my ability to think clearly and act rationally. But, most of all, it took away my freedom. First, I was a slave to my physical cravings and food thoughts, and now I'm a prisoner here, trapped by the high cost of this place.

I can't believe this. I woke up so excited about having only two weeks left and now I'm terrified of having to stay longer. If that happens, then my trip to Disney World will be ruined too. I have tried really hard not to get excited about going there when I leave because it seems so far away. But this morning I actually felt as if it was going to happen soon. I even started to think about how much fun it would be to go on all the rides without worrying if I would fit in them.

Now, all of that could be gone. Not getting to visit Disney World would be awful, but having to stay here even one second longer than six weeks would be unbearable. I have to make sure to begin "working" again so they will let me out on time. Please, God, help me.

◆ *Day 30* ◆

August 1, 1989

(13 days left)

I learned a lot on this first day of a new month. During the educational lecture in the afternoon Linda talked about feelings. She started by writing "FEELINGS ARE . . ." on the blackboard and asked us to complete the sentence. Almost everyone raised their hands with something different to say.

One person said feelings are good. Another said feelings are overwhelming, and someone said feelings are difficult and confusing. I said that feelings are wrong. Even though I knew that wasn't true, it was the first thought that came to my mind.

Growing up, I had a hard time expressing my feelings. I always thought it was wrong for me to feel sad or depressed, yet I always did, so I felt bad all of the time. First, I would get depressed. Then, I'd get angry at myself for having those feelings. And, finally, I would become obsessed with trying to control the bad feelings I thought I wasn't supposed to have.

After about fifteen minutes, someone in the group finally asked why anything had to follow the statement.

Couldn't it be a full sentence? Linda pointed out that she never said there had to be an ending, that we were the ones who put all these conditions on her statement.

The point of the lecture was just what the statement said—FEELINGS ARE. Linda said, "Feelings just are. Period. End of statement." And, for the first time, I understood exactly what she meant. I don't have any control over my feelings. No matter how hard I try, I cannot force myself to stop feeling something. Whatever I feel is beyond my control.

Linda stressed that while feelings are beyond our control, actions are not. In other words, when I used to get really angry, that was okay, but taking it out on others was not. That's how it is with my food addiction: I am powerless over the fact that I am an addict, but I am responsible for my actions if I want to remain in recovery.

I'm amazed that I finally understood some of this stuff. This was one of the first things that made sense to me. I understand that I cannot control my feelings. All those years spent trying so hard to stop what I considered to be negative feelings were in vain. My efforts probably only intensified the feelings. If I had just let them pass, they wouldn't have been nearly as painful.

I feel better after what happened yesterday. The part I didn't concentrate on after our meeting was that the psychiatrist did say everything was okay now. I have to believe what he says and pray that I will be allowed to leave on time. Now, the questions.

First, I have to reread chapter 4 of the AA Big Book, then discuss the choice presented in this chapter to believe in God and turn my life over to Him or to continue to suffer hopelessly in my disease.

Next, I have to write about how deep down inside of me there is an idea of God, then elaborate on how things have gotten in the way of my spirituality. Deep down, I have always known that God is taking care of me and is with me. The worship of food, other people, and relationships have always gotten in the way of my spirituality. I never allowed God's will to be done. I only prayed for my will to be done.

Now, I have to discuss my feelings about the quote "Who are YOU to say there is no God?" and whether I believe that as soon as I believe in God, my eating problem will no longer be a concern. No, I believe that I have to turn my life over to God each day for the strength, courage, and knowledge to remain abstinent for the next twenty-four hours. I do that every day.

Finally, I need to discuss the issues these questions raise and how they are important in my acceptance of the program: This chapter shows me my life was a mess before I began to communicate with God. This is important for me to always remember because I never want to go back to being hopeless and alone.

◄ Day 31 ►

August 2, 1989

(12 days left)

For the past several days we've been cutting out pictures of our binge foods and making a collage. Then, today, we did the weirdest thing I've ever done. Instead of having education in the afternoon, the counselors gathered us for a "food funeral."

The idea, they said, was to bury our binge foods once and for all, to say good-bye to those foods we were no longer eating. They instructed us to do this by naming out loud the foods in our collages and putting them underneath a huge, black blanket.

I was certain that I would burst out laughing. I mean, how could anyone take this seriously?

As the first few people began to list their binge foods, they became very upset when it was time to put the collages under the blanket. Some people had even been assigned to write good-bye letters to food, which they read during the funeral.

At first, I struggled to feel sympathy. I couldn't seem to get past that these people were putting pieces of paper under a blanket in the middle of a circle of other crazy people. But as Georgia began naming her foods, her moan echoed throughout the room.

She said a long good-bye to those things that have been her longtime friends, lovers, and companions. Through her tears, she talked about how much she would miss having her food around when she was lonely or sad. She said she would miss the excitement of planning and preparing to be with food. But, most of all, she would miss turning to food to celebrate the special times in her life.

"Good-bye to birthday cake and Christmas cookies," she sobbed. "Good-bye to potato chips, ice cream, and Easter chocolate. Good-bye to the wedding cake I'll never eat."

As soon as I heard her statement about the wedding cake, I felt tears well up in my eyes. I hadn't thought about that. There would be no more baking chocolate-chip cookies for Tim. Now, I'd never be able to show him just what a good wife I'd make. And what about the children I hoped to have? Would I never be able to bake cookies with them?

After Georgia had finished, I walked to the middle of the circle to bury my binge foods.

"Good-bye to bread and doughnuts. Good-bye to peanut butter and crackers," I sobbed. "Good-bye to pizza, ice cream, and Doritos. Good-bye to chocolate-chip cookies and popcorn. . . ."

I couldn't continue. It hit me that I would no longer be able to eat popcorn. There would be no more afternoons in front of the television with my popcorn smothered in butter and the soap operas. No longer would I be able to feel the crunchy kernels between my teeth as the melting butter caressed my tongue. There would be no more creamy chocolate to melt slowly in my mouth.

Sobbing, I glanced around the room at everyone else. Most of them, too, were crying. That new guy, Dave, looked confused, but the others seemed genuinely upset. Some were even bent over in pain, while a few were holding hands to console each other.

All the while I felt tears on my cheeks, but inside there was a voice telling me I was faking my grief. It said I was a phony and that I was acting, performing for a good "grade." I suddenly became terrified that one of the counselors would hear the voice too.

Quickly, I placed my pictures underneath the blanket and returned to my seat. For the next hour, I quietly listened as the others said good-bye to their binge foods. Avoiding everyone's gaze, I studied the worn carpet and prayed that the counselors weren't watching me.

When it was all over, Phil scooped up the pictures under the blanket and carried them away. Unless we chose to, he said, we would never have to eat our binge foods again. They were buried forever and as soon as we were done mourning them, we would be free. I'm still not sure what happened, but I am glad it's over.

Time for the questions so I can put an end to this strange day. It was truly the weirdest thing I've ever experienced.

◆ Day 32 ◆

August 3, 1989
(11 days left)

Just before family group, we had assertiveness training
again and I learned a lot. In one of the first sessions a
few weeks ago, I learned how to state my feelings in a
healthy way by using the "I feel _____ when you _____"
statement. Today, I learned about the characteristics of
nonassertive, assertive, and aggressive behavior.

According to the paper Linda handed out, which is
from the Center for Rational Living, nonassertive behavior is "allowing people to treat you, your thoughts and
feelings in whatever way they want without your challenging it. It means doing what others want you to do
regardless of your own desires."

Assertive behavior is "thinking and acting in ways that
stand up for your legitimate personal rights. It is the act
of giving expression to your own thoughts and feelings in
a way that defines your own human perspective without
subtracting from the legitimate human rights of others."

Aggressive behavior is "standing up for what you want
regardless of the rights and feelings of others. Aggression
can be either physical or verbal."

With nonassertive behavior, a problem is avoided, while in assertive behavior the problem is attacked. With aggressive behavior, however, it is the person who is attacked. This really hit home for me. Before I came here, I would go from nonassertive behavior to aggressive behavior, never realizing there was assertiveness.

For instance, I would always hope for things—special food from my parents, dinners out, attention from Tim—but I would never simply ask for them, which would be the healthy approach. And sometimes, as happens with aggressive behavior, I would demand things such as money and food from my parents. I never knew how to simply ask for them. I just thought everyone should know what I wanted and give it to me. That certainly put a lot of pressure on others and frustrated me.

The example that really screams out to me is one about anger. In nonassertive behavior, the person builds anger and resentment—sounds familiar—while in aggressive behavior, the anger is acted out. I went from one extreme to the other. Either I would smile and pretend everything was okay while shoving my anger down, or I would get really mad and yell and scream in a rage.

The healthy way, I learned today, is to use the assertive approach and deal with the anger. That's what I'm learning to do here. And it all comes back to that simple "I feel _____ when you _____" formula. It's amazing how quickly anger passes when it's expressed, even if it's old anger.

Today, right now, I am free of the anger and resentment I felt toward myself and it feels wonderful. I no longer hate myself because I couldn't stop eating and I'm not angry at God anymore either. I feel light and free! I didn't know it was possible to feel this way!

August 4, 1989

(10 days left)

Today during small patient group, the one where all of
Linda's patients meet together, we were talking about
ways that we hide our feelings, specifically those related
to our appearance. The group has only four other women,
so it's quite intimate.

I've always used my long hair to "hide" my weight.
My hair always had to be puffy. The higher, the better. I
truly thought that the perm and hot rollers I used in my
hair made it puffy enough to distract people from my
enormous body. That and the layers of makeup I wore
made me look like a normal person, in my mind. Before
I came here, I wouldn't dream of leaving the house without my full "mask." Some mornings it took me an hour
just to get the top half of my body ready.

Other patients have been being assigned "no makeup"
or "no hair styling," but I never thought such assignments were appropriate for me. I just thought I liked to
look nice. Now, I'm wondering about it all. I haven't
used these things to hide since I've been here. So since

it hasn't affected my work here, Linda pointed out, she isn't giving me one of those assignments. Thank God.

Still, I am considering getting my hair cut. There's a hairdresser who comes in every other Sunday. It seems like it would be a good thing to do. Now that my face isn't so round and I've been honest about my feelings, I don't feel the need to have all of that hair anymore.

◆ Day 34 ◆

August 5, 1989

(9 days left)

This was a quiet day. Weekends around here are so much better because there's no family group. Paulette and I even had some time to sit on the pier by the duck pond. It was hot, but so nice to be outside. That's really the only time I feel even halfway normal.

Sometimes, though, it is hard to see the people in front of the apartments across the street. I look at the teenagers as they're playing basketball or skateboarding and wonder whether they know how lucky they are. To be free to set their own schedules and to not have to work at living a normal life—these seem like such basic rights. After coming here, I don't think I'll ever be the same. No matter what happens with my abstinence, I doubt that I can ever forget my experience here.

There have been a few "retreads," people who return to Glenbeigh after relapsing, lately and nothing scares me more than their stories of pain. I learned a lot from Amy. She was here a few years ago, then relapsed several months ago. To hear her talk about her shame and self-hatred terrifies me. The last thing I ever want is to go back to my old life.

As miserable as my life may be in here right now, it's also the happiest I've ever felt. I never imagined that there were other people in the world who did the insane things I did with food. There hasn't been one thing I've done, right down to taking the pickles off my quarter-pounders and ordering two diet sodas, that someone here hasn't also experienced. It is truly a miracle.

In the outside world, I always felt like such a freak. A lot of it was because of my size, but there was also the obsessive relationship I had with food. I could never understand how my sister or my friends would say they were full and not eat any more. It never made sense to me when someone turned down dessert. I always had room for more food.

Until I came here, I never even knew what it felt like to be physically full and, the opposite, what true hunger felt like either. I finally know what hunger feels like. For the first few days, I wasn't sure what that rumbling in my stomach just before mealtime was. But then I heard someone else talk about feeling hungry for the first time and everything made sense. For the first time in my life, my body was reacting normally to needing food!

It was important for me to hear that you don't die from hunger. It was vital for me to understand that. At first, I was afraid of my hunger. I had the idea that I would die from the discomfort. But once I let it wash over me, I learned that I could live through it. I'm still afraid of not having enough to eat, but the weighing and measuring helps with that.

When I get scared now, I tell myself that if my cup of vegetables filled me yesterday, then it will do the same today. As much as I hate measuring my food, I can really see a reason for it. I once heard a guy say, "I can look at an entire buffet and tell myself that it's about a cup." I could really relate to that.

Today, Paulette and I were talking about going home; she's leaving next week. It amazes me that she doesn't want to. She likes it here! That's the biggest thing we disagree on. I really like her though. She seems serious about her recovery without being obsessive. She's gentle and kind. She doesn't yell and scream and I can really talk to her as I've never talked to anyone before. She doesn't judge me, even though she knows everything I've done, including my abortion. I've never known such acceptance.

She lives all the way in Montana and after we leave here, I don't know if I'll ever see her again. I don't know if I'll ever see any of these people again. It's pretty weird to think that they have played such an important part in my life and I may never even speak to them again. Today, I know that whatever happens is up to God, not me.

The questions. First, I need to read pages 50–53 in the AA Big Book, then write about the "certain simple things" that create the major changes in my way of living. Simple things like saying my affirmation have helped me to love and accept myself more and created a revolutionary change in my lifestyle.

Now, I need to write about being crushed by self-imposed crises and the feelings they promote in me. I would always have one crisis or another concerning other people—Did he love me? Are they mad at me? Why doesn't anyone ask me to go out? These promote feelings of sadness, depression, anxiety, anger, and hopelessness.

Finally, I need to discuss the issues I wish to work on and why they are important: Accepting and loving myself just the way I am without feeling guilty or wrong. This is important because I need to realize how special I am and treat myself that way.

◆ Day 35 ◆

August 6, 1989

(8 days left)

The more I go to church, the more I enjoy it. It makes me feel so safe and loved, like nothing I've ever known. It's as if when I listen to the minister and his daughter speak, I'm hearing what God has to say. He's telling me that everything will be okay. And I need to hear that, because I'm starting to get nervous about leaving.

As much I want to go home, I realized something scary on the way to church. When I walk out the doors, I go alone. While I was in the van today, I told myself that I'm not afraid to leave as long as these people and this van come with me. But they can't.

Linda already told me that during my last week here, I will need to concentrate on planning for my trip to Disney World and for what they call my "aftercare." Apparently, they've been in touch with Patti, my counselor from Syracuse, and we'll continue our sessions after I leave. I also need to find a sponsor, someone to help me with my program and work on developing a daily schedule for mealtimes and exercise. As they say here, "Failure to plan is planning to fail."

185

So I guess it's going to be a big week. I think that's why church was so comforting. I just need to remember that God will take care of me, no matter what. I've been praying for tolerance and safety, asking God to help me deal with whatever comes my way. And even though a part of me still doubts, another part has come to believe.

◆ Day 36 ◆

August 7, 1989
(7 days left)

One week from today and I'm out of here! I talked to my sister last night and she's pretty excited about our trip to Disney World too. And, once I leave here, I won't have to go to family group anymore!

For the first time since I talked to my father weeks ago, I was allowed to make a phone call during the day! At the nurses' station they have this big red notebook with listings of people who have gone through Glenbeigh. It's organized by states. Unfortunately, I didn't find too many people from Syracuse. One lady I called said she was in relapse and wouldn't make a good sponsor. That scared me a lot but I was determined not to give up.

Next, I called a man who was here a few years ago to see if he knew of anyone who would sponsor me. While I wanted desperately to ask him to be my sponsor, Linda had already told me that I needed to find a female sponsor. She said that a male sponsor, especially a single one, would distract me from my recovery.

Glenbeigh recommends not having any sort of a

romantic relationship for at least a year after leaving. The rules would, of course, be different if I were already married or involved. I'm not sure I'll listen to that suggestion. I'll have to wait and see. I mean, if Tim all of sudden decided to ask me out, I would go in a second.

I've been thinking about Tim a lot lately. I know that when I get back, we're going to be in a class together and that makes me nervous. How am I going to react when I see him after all this time? Will that be the thing that pushes me over the edge and into the food?

To say I'm nervous is an understatement. Before I left, I wrote him this embarrassing letter about how much I loved him and soon I'll have to face him. How will he act? What will he say? Will he even notice the changes in me? Will that make him love me?

I know that even though I've come a long way here, I still have many of the same feelings I did before I left. Despite my recovery, I would love nothing more than for Tim to whisk me away to a castle where we'd live happily ever after. Try as I might, I can't seem to push aside my feelings for him, even though it would be in my best interest.

If I think about him too much, I want to cry. I wanted to believe that he loved me too, yet he never did anything to make me think he did. He occasionally flirted with me, but there's a big difference between flirting and committing. I only wish that he would have done the latter. I really do love him but I'm terrified that seeing him again will destroy everything I've worked so hard for.

When I talked to Ellen about it, she asked me how long it would be until I saw him. I told her about a month. Looking directly in my eyes, she said, "Don't worry about next month. You don't even know if you'll be here tomorrow, never mind next month."

Though I laughed, part of me hated her for dismissing my feelings so flippantly. And I know I hated her because she was right. I don't know that I'll be alive in a month and I don't know that I'll ever see him. He could have dropped the class we are scheduled to be in together. I still hope that I see him though. I can't seem to help it.

And there's a side of me that really hopes Tim will ask me out so I can say no, now that I've lost all this weight. But I know I wouldn't. As much as I'd like to be able to flaunt my new body in front of him, it wouldn't work out that way. I hate myself for it, but I'm so desperate for his love that I know I would go out with him if he asked.

I better do the questions. It seems like I need all the help I can get. First, I need to read pages 54–57 in the AA book, then write a description of what my God would be like: A God who will love me no matter what I've done. One who will be there with me through good and bad times. A God I trust with my life and One who is always loving.

Next, I need to write about the things I have worshipped in my life before finding my Higher Power: Food. John. Money. Tim. My father.

Now, I need to discuss the great reality deep down inside of me and determine whether it works. The great reality within me is that God is in me. Yes, that really works. I came to this conclusion a few days ago when Kathy read her God-wanted ad. I felt God's presence inside of me.

Finally, I need to write about the issues that the idea of God within me raises: Turning my will *completely* over to Him without telling or asking Him for what I want. I just keep saying, "Thy will be done not mine," and the God within me gives me the strength I need.

◆ Day 37 ◆

August 8, 1989
(6 days left)

I felt such a sense of accomplishment today. After several weeks of working on my ceramic heart in recreation group, I got to take it back to my room. The ceramic piece is a heart-shaped dish with a lid. I painted it white and put a big, yellow cross on the top. The lid doesn't fit perfectly and the cross is crooked, but I love it. I've never made anything like it before.

I'm coming to realize just how much of my life was spent eating, thinking about food, or planning to eat. It's sad to think about all that I could have accomplished if I hadn't been so deep into my disease.

One of the first things they gave me here was a chart outlining the characteristics of food addiction and recovery. It's sketched in a U-shape. The left side tells about an addict's descent into the disease, while the right side describes recovery. On the left side, during the critical phase, it says that a person loses interest in anything besides food. That sure applies to my life. I don't think I've ever really had a hobby except for eating and cooking.

I never understood getting involved in extracurricular

191

activities. I could have cared less about doing such things
and I certainly didn't want to be around other people. It
took too much work to keep up the appearance of always
being happy. And, besides, the more time I spent with
people, the more chance there was of them teasing me.
School was enough of an ordeal for me. Looking at my
heart dish, it's amazing that I could create such a thing.
I know it's far from perfect, but for the first time in my
life, that doesn't matter. What counts is that I had the
courage to actually make it. And I was afraid. Before I actually painted the cross on the lid, I tried to get someone
else to do it, but no one would. Now, I'm glad for that. I
wouldn't feel this good looking at it if someone else had
made it.

I had some time to talk with the new guy, Dave, today.
He seems really nice. He's from Maryland and very shy.
We didn't have too much to say to each other except to
make fun of the rules here. He thinks it's ridiculous to
need a buddy when he goes outside to smoke. It was kind
of nice to talk to someone different. It's been mostly the
same people for weeks.

I also met with Linda today. It was our final individual
meeting. She handed me an assignment sheet that was
like no other. It included preparation sheets for the aftercare work I need to get done before I leave. It's really important because I heard that if you don't finish this stuff,
they keep you here until you do.

The first thing I have to do is outline a month's worth
of schedules for after I leave. The schedules must include
exercise times, mealtimes, support group meetings, and
sleep time to make sure I don't forget to do any of them.
She also said that I need to attend the aftercare group
this Wednesday and participate in the field trip to the
grocery store on that day.

In addition, I need to find a sponsor by Friday. She says that all of these things will help alleviate the fear I have of transition by "developing structured and viable aftercare plans." I certainly hope so. How am I even going to have time to worry about my transition into the outside world?

August 9, 1989

(5 days left)

Right after lunch today, I went on my grocery store out-ing. Lisa, a volunteer here, guided us through an enor-mous food store. Walking in the door, I was overwhelmed by the smells that filled the air, but since I had just eaten lunch, I was full. That helped a lot.

The first thing Lisa said was that at most groceries, the items we need will be in the outside aisles of the store. Fruits and vegetables, meats, dairy, and frozen produce are usually kept in the perimeters of stores. She said that, with the exception of condiments and cereal, there will be no need to go down the other aisles.

"It's not a good idea to go down the baking aisle. Stay away from it no matter what. You have no business down there," she said firmly. "Why torture yourself with seeing things you can't eat? You wouldn't expect an alcoholic to go into a bar just to look around, would you?"

We shook our heads. Lisa then led us to the condi-ment aisle. Here, she explained, we are allowed to have any salad dressing, salsa, tomato sauce, mayonnaise,

195

mustard, ketchup, barbecue sauce, and soy sauce that doesn't have sugar listed in the first four ingredients.

Only three other people were in the group, but it took Lisa almost fifteen minutes to get through just the condiments. Everyone, except for Michelle, who remained calm and business-like, was so paranoid. It was as if their fear blocked them from listening to what Lisa was saying. They kept asking the same questions. I just wanted to scream. Lisa handled everyone well though.

After that, the tour got easier. Lisa took us to the soda aisle and told us not to turn around. Grocery stores usually situate the soda across from the snacks. This means that every time I go to buy soda, I will be faced with seeing my biggest binge foods. God help me.

We can have any kind of soda that doesn't contain sugar or caffeine. That includes a chocolate-flavored one. Lisa said that while some people can drink this soda, others can't deal with tasting chocolate.

"If a red flag goes up in your mind, then you need to listen to that," she said. "Though you may not want to admit it, you will always know when something is going to be a problem for you. I, personally, can't drink anything that tastes like chocolate, but some people can."

The minute she said chocolate, I could see that red flag she talked about go up. I don't think I'll even try it. Around here they say, "When in doubt, leave it out."

After that, Lisa brought us to the meat and dairy cases. She said to try to buy the leanest cuts of meat that we can. Eighty-five percent fat-free ground beef is great, she pointed out. For dairy items, she showed us the skim milk, nonfat yogurt, cottage cheese, and ricotta cheese.

Our next stop was the cereal aisle. There, Lisa showed us how most of the cereals we eat will either be at the end of the aisle or on the bottom shelves. Without any sugar or flour in them, these items aren't best-sellers, so they are placed out of the way.

At the checkout stand, Lisa said it is okay to have sugar-free gum, but cough drops and candies without sugar are too easy to binge on.

I hadn't had any gum since I got here. I used to shove one piece after another in my mouth while I was doing homework. Chewing it long enough to get the flavor out, I would then stuff a fresh piece in, continuing until I had gone through at least two packs.

When Lisa said we could buy gum and chew up to six pieces a day, I told Michelle that I wanted to try chewing gum again, but I was worried.

"Why don't you try having only three pieces of gum at first. Have one after each meal and I'll hold the pack for you," she said firmly.

Nodding, I purchased two packs of strawberries and cream sugarless bubble gum. After opening one pack and taking a piece, I handed the rest to Michelle. Unwrapping the piece, I was terrified that this stupid little piece of gum would set me off.

I said a silent prayer about God's will being done and not mine. As the sweetness of the small cube of gum melted in my mouth, I slowly bit down on the lusciously flavored block. How wonderful it was to feel the familiar rubberiness between my teeth as small, soft bubbles formed with each bite.

By the time Lisa directed us back into the van, however, the novelty of the gum had worn off. While I still enjoyed chewing it, without the sugary taste, there was no high from this gum. The first thing I did when I returned to Glenbeigh was to throw out my gum.

We got back just in time for one of my favorite things, "coining," when patients who are leaving are presented with a copper-colored coin as a symbol of completing treatment. I was doubly excited because both Paulette and I were receiving coins today.

Her individual counselor, Theo, presented Paulette with the coin, saying that she was grateful to have met such a gentle soul so.committed to recovery. Then, Phil talked about how much Paulette had grown since she first came here. He said that she had really learned to express her feelings and to have fun. As the counselors were speaking, I started to cry. Paulette was leaving tomorrow and I hated to see her go.

Next, Linda presented me with my coin. She said that she felt blessed watching my growth and that we had grown together. As one of her first patients, I would always be special to her, she said.

Then Phil spoke and said he knew exactly when the turning point in my recovery came. It was at someone else's First Step. Everyone had been saying nice things to the person who had shared, but then I raised my hand and talked about the self-pity I'd heard. It was the first time that I hadn't simply spoken about how I related to the person's experience. I had given genuine feedback.

Then he said he was going to miss me. My eyes filled with tears as I walked up to Linda to get my coin.

"You're going to have an exciting life," she whispered in my ear as she hugged me tightly. "Good luck."

Everyone clapped as my eyes filled with tears of gratitude.

As if all of this wasn't enough for one day, I also attended the aftercare group. Though I was nervous at first, it really wasn't hard. We mostly talked about what was going on in everyone's life. The people who lived at the hospital's halfway house for food addiction also attended this meeting. It was nice to hear about their experiences and to know that people really can live abstinently in the outside world. I need to remember this over the next several days.

August 10, 1989

(4 days left)

Today was one of the saddest days I've had here, yet it was also filled with progress. Paulette left today. I can't even say how much I wanted to go with her. She's been here since I first came. I can't imagine it here without her. So many of the people who were here when I started have left. There's so many new people that I don't feel like I belong here anymore.

Last night, I gave Paulette one of the twin teddy bears my parents sent me a few weeks ago. I had planned to give her the dark brown and keep the tan one so we would each have a reminder of the other, but before I could, she actually asked for the brown one. I was so proud of her that she could do that. It took a lot of courage.

I've never had a friend like Paulette and I'm not ready to lose her. We promised to keep in touch and I truly hope that we do. When I came here, I never imagined that I would meet such a good friend, and now I'm having a hard time imagining life without her. It will be strange to wake up tomorrow and not see Paulette.

I was able to find a sponsor today. Her name is Jane

and she lives in Syracuse. We didn't have a lot of time to talk but she seemed really nice. She offered to pick me up at the airport and go grocery shopping with me for the first time. What a relief! I am so terrified of walking into the grocery store alone. Since I'm flying back to Syracuse, my family won't be there to help. Who would have thought that I would need help with something as simple as grocery shopping? This is just one small example of the way my life has drastically changed.

I also met with Paulette's counselor, Theo, to discuss my trip to Disney World. Linda told me that Theo had been there while abstinent, so she could help me. The first suggestion Theo had was to call the hotel and request a refrigerator in my room. I would need that to store my breakfast and snack foods.

"You can't really go into a restaurant and find nonfat, plain yogurt or sugar- and flour-free cereal," she pointed out. "You'll need to store these things in your room. I found it much easier to eat those two meals in my room when I went. For lunch and dinner, you can usually find what you need. Most places have salad, plain meat, steamed vegetables, and a baked potato."

Theo also suggested that I buy a few items at the grocery store. Since I can have a baked potato only three times a week, I need to bring a starch with me for lunch and some dinners. Corn, chickpeas, or kidney beans are good choices, she said. Bringing salad dressing would be a good idea too, she said.

After our meeting, I was allowed to call the hotel. It would be no problem to get a small refrigerator in the room. Theo had told me to say it was for medical reasons, because in reality it is.

As I get ready to do the questions, I am thinking about Paulette. By now she's had time to eat at least one, if not two, meals away from here. I hope it's going well for her. I remember hearing about this one guy who had to call his counselor from the bus station because he wanted to eat so badly once he got out there. He made it okay. I just hope Paulette is as blessed.

◆ *Day 40* ◆

August 11, 1989

(3 days left)

I feel like such a fool. I did something I never would have done before coming here. In small patient group, I admitted that I have started to have feelings for that new guy, Dave. I know we only talked for a few minutes, but I think he's really cute. I said that I was afraid my feelings would interfere with my recovery.

To deal with my feelings, the people in the group and Linda suggested that I tell Dave how I feel. I was mortified! In the past, the only way I'd ever been able to tell a guy that I cared about him was in writing. I never had the guts to actually talk to anyone face-to-face about what I felt. I was always afraid that any guy I said those words to would laugh in my face or say something mean about my weight.

Well, with the group's encouragement and only a few more days before the decision about whether I get to leave, I decided to tell Dave how I feel. I asked Ellen if she would come with me and she agreed. Even though Ellen is great, I miss Paulette more than ever. I know she would have been wonderful during all of this.

After dinner and before the group meeting, I saw Dave coming out of the smoking room. With a final look in Ellen's direction, I approached him. My heart pounded and I wanted to run far away. I had no idea why I had agreed to such a stupid suggestion. Pulling him aside in the far corner of the lounge where no one else could hear, I fumbled over my words as I searched for the right thing to say.

"Can I talk to you for a minute?" My voice was shaky. After he nodded, I continued. "Dave . . . I . . . uh . . . I need to tell you something."

I hesitated, taking a deep breath and grasping for the right words. Finally, I whispered, "I'm starting to have these feelings for you and I just wanted you to know." I looked at the floor, then slowly up at him. His face was deep red.

"I . . . I uh . . . I just mean that I think you're really nice." I forced myself to look at him and smile.

After what seemed like an eternity, he looked down at the floor and said, "I don't know what to say . . . I . . . Thank you." He smiled.

As we stood there, I was relieved to be interrupted by a group of people walking toward the meeting.

"Oh, I better get going. . . . The meeting and every-thing. . . ." I fumbled over my words and quickly walked away to the safety of my room and Ellen.

After a few minutes of discussion, I told Ellen that I didn't want to talk about it anymore. It was over and done with. There was nothing I could do. And what hope was there anyway? Dave lived in Maryland and I was leaving in three days. It was just one of those things that wasn't meant to be, but the important thing is that I had the courage to state my feelings.

I still feel really foolish. When I talked to him, I

couldn't even seem to get the words out straight. I felt so clumsy and awkward. And I still wish Paulette were here to talk with. She would know just what to say. I really hope she's okay out there without any of us to turn to.

Since she left, I've spent some time wondering what it'll be like when I leave. I know that the first week will be strange because of going to Disney World, but what about when I get back to Syracuse?

Mark, Wendy, and most of my other friends will be gone. Other than Tim and one or two additional people, there won't really be anyone I know. They all graduated while I was in here. By now, they're just about ready to leave Syracuse.

I'm afraid that I'll be so lonely without my friends there. Never again do I want to experience that awful loneliness that I've finally gotten rid of. While the logical part of me knows that the loneliness came from being so isolated in my addiction, it's still hard to forget how painful it was.

◆ Day 41 ◆

August 12, 1989
(2 days left)

I'm really looking forward to seeing my sister and going
to Disney World, but I am so afraid. I keep wondering
what I've done to myself by scheduling this trip. It
seemed like such a good idea before I came here. Now,
it seems like a huge obstacle to my recovery.

When I think about all of the food at Disney World,
I feel overwhelmed with fear. How am I going to react
to seeing other people eating things I can't have? I'm
so afraid to lose what I've found here. Never have I been
happier, more at ease, and saner. It seems like a contra-
diction to say that I'm sane while I'm locked up in this
place, yet it's true.

My life has changed completely and I'm sane enough
to be able to notice it. One of the biggest miracles is that
I don't hate myself today. It used to be so painful to look
in the mirror. I hated who I saw so much; today I can
even stand naked in front of myself. At my size, that's
amazing to me.

The strangest thing is that I came here solely to lose
weight. That was all that mattered. I didn't care about

209

expressing my feelings or being healthy. All I wanted, like I so desperately had prayed for my entire life, was to be thin. I truly believed that if I lost weight, my entire life would change and I'd be incredibly happy.

The thing is that I have probably lost only twenty or so pounds and I'm incredibly happy. Losing weight doesn't matter so much anymore. While I like it that I am, the important things in my life today can't be measured on the scale.

For the first time in my life, I know the meaning of such words as *honesty, dignity, self-respect,* and *self-esteem.* Before I came here, these were just trite words people tossed around when they wanted you to see things their way. Today, they are some of the most important words I've ever known.

There truly are not words to express the gratitude I feel. That someone as hopeless as I once was could feel the peace I do makes me believe that there has to be a God. Only He could create such a miracle.

I finally completed my weekly plan sheets for after I leave Disney World. On Sunday, August 20, my plane arrives in Syracuse at 5:00 P.M. My new sponsor and I will go shopping; then I'll have dinner and go to a support group meeting. The next few days will be kind of restful. I have an appointment with my counselor on Tuesday at 5:30; then on Wednesday I'm leaving to go home.

I've already talked to my parents about what I'll need to eat, and they were wonderful. Between my mom and dad, they said they'd get me everything I need. I learned in here that just because they're my parents doesn't mean they are responsible for taking care of me. My food plan is my responsibility, but I am grateful for their help, especially after the five-hour drive I'll have.

My mealtimes will stay pretty much the same. I plan

to eat breakfast at nine, lunch at one, dinner at six, and snack at ten. I figured I would exercise after breakfast and go to support group meetings in the evenings. I've also learned from my new sponsor that there's a Unity Church in Syracuse and I plan to go on Sundays.

The following week when I'm back in school, my schedule will be different. Since most of my classes are at 1:00, I'll have to eat breakfast at 8:30 and lunch at noon. After breakfast, I'll exercise and I'll eat dinner at 6:00 P.M. With support group meetings and counseling in the evenings, I'll be pretty busy. Then, at 10:00 P.M., I'll eat my snack and go to bed after I shower.

It's truly amazing to me that I have all of this planned out. Six weeks ago, I barely got up in time for my 1:00 P.M. classes and now, here I am grateful that I'll be able to sleep until 8:30 after all of this time of getting up at 6:00 A.M.

I had better get working on the questions. First, they want me to read Step 4, then discuss the qualities that I like most and least about myself. I like my smile, my friendliness, the way I can be honest with others even when I don't want to be, my willingness, and my spirituality. I don't like my ego, my pride, my controlling and manipulating manner, and the way I beat up on myself.

Now, I need to list the fears I have about changing the things I like the least about myself: I'm afraid to give up control even though logically I know I never had any. It's still scary to give up my will and trust God.

Finally, I need to explore how I feel after looking at the qualities I like about myself and discuss how I will build on these qualities: Happiness. By staying abstinent and working the program; praying to God and turning to others.

August 13, 1989

(1 day left)

I did it. This morning I had my hair cut, about three inches off the back and a good amount off the top. When I look in the mirror, I can see my face. I feel kind of naked.

On the other hand, I feel as if I've lost hundreds of pounds of baggage. I now have the freedom to wear my hair in any style I want. If I chose to, I can stop using hot rollers. My head feels so light and free. It's wonderful!

So many people complimented me on my haircut. Even Linda said how nice it looks. For once, I believed what they were saying. And I believed them when they told me that I've lost a lot of weight. I feel it. Tomorrow before I leave, I'll find out exactly how much.

I'm so excited about leaving! In less than twenty-four hours, I'll be out of here. And I'm ready. Even though I am scared, I know it's time. As much as I hated it here, this is an extremely safe place. There is no food here that I can't eat.

I know it's completely different in the outside world. One of the things they've made me realize here is that, though our disease is similar to alcoholism, society's treatment of our substance is completely opposite. As someone in here said, "No one has ever been arrested for driving under the influence of Twinkies."

From the minute I walk out that door, I'll be assaulted with signs encouraging me to eat luscious treats. There will be strong food smells at the airport, and during my hour drive to Orlando, I'll be tempted by billboards and radio advertisements encouraging me to "take a break" or "have just one." Unlike alcoholics, who may go for days without seeing their substance, there isn't a place in this world that I can go where food isn't present.

Alcohol and drugs are seen as evil, while food is thought to be comforting. How many commercials have I seen encouraging mothers to bake some love for their children? What is it they tell us, "Feed a cold, starve a fever"?

I've come to realize that besides changing my eating habits, I have to change my entire outlook on life. I can no longer feed anything. No amount of baked goods will make me feel love for myself. I can't "take a break" that involves eating fast food, and I'll never be able to celebrate a birthday by eating cake. Who thought of that anyway?

During my time here and by writing all of this, I have learned that a crucial part of my recovery has to be keeping food in its place. Food is not meant to be my friend, lover, or companion when I'm lonely. It is not intended to be a reward or punishment. Food is not a cure-all for everything that goes wrong in my life and it can't make me feel better. It is simply meant to nourish my body, nothing more and nothing less.

◄ Day 43 ►

August 14, 1989
(This is it!)

This is it! This is my final entry. It's just before lunch and I'm ready to leave. I packed everything, I got my money out of the safe, and I did laundry yesterday. Right after lunch, the driver will bring me to the airport, where I'll drive a rental car to Orlando to meet my sister. It's been six weeks since I've driven a car. I hope everything goes okay.

This morning was the last time I had to get up at 6:00 A.M. Thank God! And I found out that I've lost 22½ pounds! I now weigh 305½ pounds! That means in no time I'll be out of the 300s! I never even dreamed that would be possible anytime soon. Thank you, God!

It's sort of strange knowing that I'm about to eat my last meal here. They're giving me a dinner to take with me, but this is the last time I'm going to sit in those chairs as a patient. I don't need to have a buddy to walk to the cafeteria, and I'll be able to walk out the front door by myself.

There's really not much else to write. Family group was really nice today. Everyone told me how I had helped their recoveries. Even Phil said he learned how to share his feelings in a gentler way from me. I couldn't believe that. I mean, he's the lead counselor here and he learned something from me. What an incredible thing to hear! I only wish Paulette had been here to share in my excitement.

Now, for the last time, I'm going to do the questions. First, they want me to reread Step 4, then write about the idea that outer conditions drove me to eat. I used everything as an excuse to eat: when I had an abortion, when John broke up with me, when Tim didn't love me, when someone was mean to me, and when I was unhappy.

Now, I need to write about the three most dangerous feelings for an addict. Resentment, self-pity, and unwarranted pride are all excuses for me to eat. If I hold in anger, feel sorry for myself, or feel too good or too bad, I will eat.

What I need to remember as I walk out that door is that I do not go alone. In this place, I met people who will love me no matter what happens, and I take the memory of each person with me. But, most of all, my life is now guided by a loving God who will protect me as long as I'm willing to accept His help. Thank You, God.

Epilogue

It's been more than thirteen years since I first walked through the doors of Glenbeigh Hospital. My stay there was and continues to be the most life-changing event I have ever experienced. And while there have been many challenges in my life since that warm August day when I left, there has not been anything or anyone worth breaking my abstinence over.

With the help of a Power greater than myself and the wonderful people I met both in treatment and since, I have achieved and continued to maintain a 160-pound weight loss. Thirteen years later, I still follow the same food plan I first received at Glenbeigh.

The night before I returned to classes, I was so terrified of seeing Tim again that I called almost anyone I could think of from treatment. And, thankfully, I found Diana. I will be forever grateful to her for talking me out of what could have been my first binge. She will never know how much she helped me.

And the next day when I saw Tim, it wasn't as traumatic as I had feared it would be. We were polite to each other and even grew to be real friends during the course of our class together. Today, I have no contact with him and am able to wish him nothing but happiness.

I have also continued to develop more open and honest relationships with the people in my life, including my parents, sister, and brother. Today, I love them in a way I didn't know possible. And I am grateful that they have all continued to be incredibly supportive of my program and my recovery.

During my first several months after leaving Disney World, I was terrified to weigh and measure my food in a restaurant without having thirty other people do so too. But, with the help and understanding of my parents, I learned that if I am persistent, I will find what I need and I can weigh and measure in even the best restaurants. Now, I go out to dinner with my parents and siblings on a regular basis and continue to weigh and measure my food without exception.

When I returned to live with my parents for a short time after my graduation, I realized that my hatred of my grandmother had really been my own self-hatred. I had blamed her for everything wrong in my life when it was really the symptoms of my disease that I hated so much.

Shortly before she died, I was able to apologize to her for all of the times that I treated her coldly. Today, I know she is up in Heaven looking down on me with love, the same love I feel for her.

After I graduated from Syracuse University, I moved back to Connecticut, and after a year of looking, found a wonderful job as a senior writer at a nonprofit environmental organization. And though there were a few challenging times—a weeklong conference in Washington and various business meetings—I was always able to work it out so that I could follow my food plan.

After a few years of working there, I decided to devote a good portion of my time to writing. My goal was to finally finish a book, something I never could have imagined accomplishing while bingeing. With the help of my family, and a lot of sacrificing, I finished writing my first book (*Why Can't I Stop Eating?* Hazelden 2000). The one you are reading is the third I have completed. Never in my life did I dream this would be possible. And though I don't know what will happen to my second manuscript, I can understand that just the act of completing even one book is a miracle.

Several years ago, I returned to Glenbeigh, not as a patient but as an employee. With increasing financial troubles, the hospital decided to set up satellite offices across the country. I was fortunate enough to be chosen as a representative in Connecticut.

As I walked through those doors again, knowing I was no longer a patient, I was still overwhelmed by the fear that I wouldn't be allowed to leave. A week of the training was more than enough for me to remember how far I'd come and I was certainly ready to return home.

Despite all of our efforts, however, things didn't turn around for Glenbeigh. One of the saddest things I've ever experienced was the closing of the hospital. In July 1993, Glenbeigh Hospital closed its doors forever. Severe financial problems stemming from drastic cuts in insurance coverage for in-patient hospitalization had forced it to close.

Though I have had contact with several of the counselors—Phil, Theo, and Donna—my heart aches for those food addicts who will never be allowed to experience the miracle I found at Glenbeigh.

Several years ago, I was lucky enough to see some of the people I was in treatment with, including Paulette.

Even after six years of not spending any time together, I was still as comfortable with her as ever. She is doing well, and there isn't a week that goes by that I don't think about her and the other people who touched my life so deeply.

Perhaps the biggest miracle I have experienced since leaving Glenbeigh comes in the form of an incredible partnership with a wonderful man. After my year of not dating was up, I desperately tried to find a romantic partner, even going so far as to place a personal ad. But God had other plans.

When I had given up trying to control the situation, I found Fred. The funny thing is, I didn't have to go far. He was right under my nose. He is the son of the woman who sponsored me at the time. Not only does he understand my food plan, but he has lived with it through his mother. There truly couldn't be a more perfect, supportive person in my life.

Five years after we met, we were joined together as husband and wife. Sitting at the head table, I weighed and measured my food as usual and did not eat even one crumb of wedding cake.

Everything I have in my life today depends on keeping my sanity, which means abstaining from sugar and flour. While that used to be a burden, it is now an incredible gift. At least I know what I need to do and today I have a choice about my actions. I choose abstinence.

Resources

Overeaters Anonymous
World Service Office
P.O. Box 44020
Rio Rancho, NM 87174-4020
(505) 891-2664
(505) 891-4320 (fax)
www.overeatersanonymous.org
E-mail: info@overeatersanonymous.org

ACORN Food Dependency Recovery Services (Week- to
Year-Long Programs around the Country)
(610) 831-5767
www.foodaddiction.com

Turning Point of Tampa (Treatment Center)
6227 Sheldon Road
Tampa, Florida 33615
(800) 397-3006
(813) 885-6974 (fax)
www.tpoftampa.com

About the Author

A recovering food addict, Debbie Danowski, Ph.D., has maintained an over 160-pound weight loss for more than thirteen years. As an alumnus of a food-addiction treatment center, Dr. Danowski has consistently used the recovery program outlined in her first book, *Why Can't I Stop Eating?*, to enjoy the benefits offered by starvation methods and diet pills, without the dangerous health risks.

Professionally, Dr. Danowski has written more than one hundred articles for national and local publications, including *First for Women, Woman's Day,* and *Seventeen.* She has also spoken at countless meetings, seminars, and conferences about food addiction, including Food Addiction 2000, the first national conference held on the disease.

Currently, Dr. Danowski is an assistant professor of English at Sacred Heart University in Fairfield, Connecticut and a member of the university's eating disorders prevention team. Dr. Danowski earned her Ph.D. at Capella University in Minneapolis, Minnesota, where she studied food representation in film. Dr. Danowski also has a master's degree in public communications with an emphasis in television, radio, and film from Syracuse University and is a member of the American Society of Journalists and Authors.